A Complete Guide
to Rubrics

A Complete Guide to Rubrics

Assessment Made Easy for Teachers of K–College

Second Edition

Audrey M. Quinlan

ROWMAN & LITTLEFIELD EDUCATION
A division of
ROWMAN & LITTLEFIELD PUBLISHERS, INC.
Lanham • New York • Toronto • Plymouth, UK

Published by Rowman & Littlefield Education
A division of Rowman & Littlefield Publishers, Inc.
A wholly owned subsidary of The Rowman & Littlefield Publishing Group, Inc.
4501 Forbes Boulevard, Suite 200, Lanham, Maryland 20706
http://www.rowmaneducation.com

Estover Road, Plymouth PL6 7PY, United Kingdom

British Library Cataloguing in Publication Information Available

Library of Congress Cataloging-in-Publication Data

Quinlan, Audrey M., 1945–
    A complete guide to rubrics : assessment made easy for teachers of K–college /
Audrey M. Quinlan. — 2nd ed.
        p. cm.
    Includes index.
    ISBN 978-1-60709-673-3 (cloth : alk. paper)—ISBN 978-1-60709-674-0 (pbk. : alk.
paper)—ISBN 978-1-60709-675-7 (ebook)
    1. Grading and marking (Students)—Handbooks, manuals, etc.   I. Title.
    LB3060.37.Q56 2011
    371.27'2—dc23   2011034789

Printed in the United States of America

To Matthew, Ryan, and Owen
who continue to amaze me "beyond expectations!"

Contents

Preface

In the educational world of using rubrics for assessment, I have found three types of teachers: those who use rubrics for *all* of their subjective assignments, those who *never* use rubrics and prefer to "grade with their gut" concerning subjective assessments, and those new teachers who are just *not sure* what a rubric is and why it matters. This work is aimed at all three groups.

A Complete Guide to Rubrics: Assessment Made Easy for Teachers K–College, Second Edition, will provide reluctant rubric users and novices with a foundation and examples of practical rubrics use. Ardent rubric users who want to provide research-based evidence for rubric use, to teach others about rubrics, to connect developmental and educational theories from kindergarten through adult education to rubric use, or simply to improve their rubric tools will also find answers in this book.

The book is designed so that each chapter can stand alone, and readers can select which chapters meet their specific needs. In addition to chapters devoted to specific grade levels from primary grades through adult education, there is a new chapter on using rubrics with students who have special needs and an updated technology chapter. There are also chapters on student-generated rubrics and adapting rubrics use to real-world grades. The appendix includes teacher-tested rubric websites.

When I began this book, my goal was to create a practical rubric handbook for educators from elementary through college levels. I sent out a call for sample rubrics to a wide variety of teachers across the United States. As expected, I received many excellent examples from teachers of all grade levels and subjects. Many of these are included throughout the text.

From this collection of scoring rubrics, I have determined that rubrics are similar to urban legends: good ones tend to spread quickly, and original sources are difficult to trace. With that in mind, I have attempted to credit original sources wherever possible. I invite readers to share their rubric experiences with me as we continue to work for impartial and explicit assessment procedures for all students.

Acknowledgments

The updated revision of this book would not have been possible without the contributions and input of a variety of talented educators. These include my colleagues at Seton Hill University, who responded positively to my call for rubrics and comments. These generous professors include: Dr. Terry Brino-Dean, Dr. Eric Cooper, Dr. David Droppa, Ms. Kaye Fierle, Dr. Daniel Gray, Sister Victoria Gribschaw, Dr. Dennis Jerz, Dr. Cynthia Magistro, Dr. Stu Thompson, and Ms. Doreen Tracy. A special thank you to Dr. Mary Ann Gawelek, Provost and Dean of the Faculty, who willingly granted "time to write," and to my education students, who provided feedback and encouragement.

Teachers and administrators from a variety of school districts throughout the nation provided rubrics for this book. My special thanks to Rose Dvorchak, Lorraine Hoffmann, Ray Rakvic, Sue Whittaker of Norwin (Pennsylvania) School District; to Lynn Quinlan and Tina McGaskill of Sumter School (South Carolina) District; to Tara Willenbrock of Fairfax County (Virginia) Schools, to Dr. Heidi Lewandowski of Southmoreland (Pennsylvania) School District, to Michele Kingsland-Smith from Franklin, Massachusetts, schools, and to all who so graciously granted permission to use their work

I am also grateful to the folks at Rowman and Littlefield, especially Tom Koerner, who took a chance on a rookie writer many years ago. My husband, Tim, deserves more than gratitude for listening, reading, typing and retyping the figures, and for never complaining.

Chapter 1

What Is a Rubric
and Why Bother?

I can't explain it. It just wasn't an A paper.

—High School English Teacher

If you've ever said, thought, or even heard a statement similar to the one uttered above by an anonymous English teacher and felt a bit uncomfortable with the comment, then this book is for you. You are not alone. When groups of teachers are asked if anyone ever questioned a grade that the teachers had assigned, or if they, themselves, had ever questioned a grade that they had received, almost every hand goes up.

Assessing and evaluating student work has become more difficult as we move into authentic learning experiences based on state and national standards. Creating rubrics for these difficult assessments—at all levels—can help teachers save time and "grading grief" (all those concerns of fairness and accuracy that plague teachers as they assess student work).

This chapter establishes the foundation of a working definition of a rubric in education, presents the ways you may already be using mental rubrics without knowing it, and explores the history of rubrics. Why teachers use rubrics in the classroom, and what research tells us about rubrics and grading, including how the use of scoring and instructional rubrics supports various learning theories, are also presented.

WHAT IS A RUBRIC?

The Concise Oxford Dictionary of English Etymology (Hoad, 1993) lists seven definitions for the term *rubric*, while the Thorndike-Barnhart (1976) dictionary lists three. The definitions range from "headings in a book; rules or directions; a short commentary on a broad subject" to "red ochre."

1

Which one of the 10 definitions is the educational one? Once again, education has created its own definition. Although the rules and directions definition comes the closest to the definition that supports the use of rubrics in the classroom, it doesn't clearly define the way teachers use rubrics.

However, the very general definitions of a scoring rubric as "guidelines for scoring a response" (NEA, 1993, p. 95) and the "criteria for assessing . . . complicated things" (Arter and McTighe, 2001, p. 5) more precisely define the use of rubrics in today's classrooms. In other words, rubrics help us to make the decisions needed to evaluate and assess.

RUBRICS IN OUR DAILY LIVES

Whether they know it or not, people create rubrics—guidelines for decisions for evaluation and assessment—in their minds every day. We each make hundreds of daily decisions: Paper or plastic? Credit or debit? Dress up or dress down? Fries with that? If someone needs paper bags to create a book cover, they'll answer paper; if they are counting carbs or fats, they may say "no, thank you" to the fries offer; and if they know that they have a parent conference scheduled for after school, they may elect not to participate in the dress-down day.

These "mental rubrics" help us to make decisions based on both our prior knowledge and current objectives. Most people also use mental rubrics to assess a variety of situations. Driving down the expressway, a driver may mentally evaluate fellow drivers based on their maneuvers. Interestingly enough, these drivers seldom are praised with a reaction of "good job" but are usually assessed on the basis of their lack of care and consideration.

However, in a restaurant, diners often mentally compare their meal and service to prior experiences whether in that same restaurant or in another place. Consider this actual scenario: A couple walked into their favorite mid-priced restaurant with their expectations (known as "benchmarks" in rubric-speak) in place. These areas of expectations included atmosphere, service, price, quality, and quantity of food.

As soon as they were seated, they began to notice some differences. There were flies around their booth, and they never had seen flies in this restaurant previously. The menu had changed, but they knew that restaurants often do that and it can be a good thing. They were pleased to see that their favorite dishes were still listed, and although the prices had increased by a dollar or two, they knew that so had the prices of many other commodities.

Upon ordering, they were told that they could no longer substitute soup for salad. And as for the final items in their mental rubric, quality and quantity, the restaurant had reduced the number of shrimp on the seafood platter! Knowing how their favorite eatery had changed and assessing those changes based on prior experiences, they said that they probably would not go back for a while—at least not until it was too cold for flies. Although they did not assign a letter grade, they did evaluate and assess.

As educators, we also make daily decisions based on our prior experiences with student work. A veteran middle school teacher remembered when one of his former students stopped in to visit after about six weeks as a ninth grader in the local high school. An A student in eighth grade, Michelle was dismayed that she could not seem to earn an A on her writing assignments for her ninth-grade English teacher. Since the middle school teacher had taught a writing workshop with this student and knew the quality of her work, he began to quiz her: "What are the comments on your papers? Have you approached the teacher about this?"

The student's answer will make effective teachers shake their heads and effective principals weep. "There are no marks on my paper except a B at the top. When I asked the teacher why it was a B, he said, 'I can't explain it. It just wasn't an A paper, Michelle. Keep trying.'"

Obviously, Mr. Marks (not his real name), an experienced teacher, had his standards—his own mental rubric—for grading each writing assignment. What Mr. Marks didn't know was that by taking the time to write down his mental rubric and communicating that information to his students, he would be able to eliminate vague comments like, "I can't explain it. It just wasn't an A paper." And in this litigious society of accountability, it just makes sense for educators to document, document, document. Using scoring rubrics will help you to provide that documentation.

HISTORY OF SCORING RUBRICS

Some of us remember teaching before scoring rubrics became an educational buzzword, but the term has been around for centuries. The etymology of the word *rubric* is unique and involved. Etymologists tell us that our use of the term *rubric* comes originally from Middle French *rubrique*, literally, "red ocher," and from the Latin *rubrica*, ultimately from the Latin *ruber*, "red."

The term *rubric* was originally used in Middle English to name red ocher, a red pigment. In ancient Rome, the citizens called a law a *rubric* because it was written with red pigment, and, at one time, headings in books were in red and also known as rubrics.

Yet in present-day English, *rubric* is used to mean "an authoritative rule" or "an explanatory commentary." The transition from using the term *rubric* to mean the color red to criteria for assessing is simple to follow. Centuries ago, authors and printers put instructions or explanations in a manuscript or printed book in red ink to contrast with the black ink of the text. Also, in religious services, the directions for the clerics in all liturgical books (missals and hymnals) were designated by the red ink used to differentiate the directions or movements from the prayers and texts and were called a *rubric* (All Words, 2004; Ruby aggregator, 2004; *Webster's New Encyclopedic Dictionary*, 2002).

Even today in the Catholic Church, the various books for rituals use red ink to tell the priest or deacon when to do certain things. A priest described this use of a rubric: "It is somewhat odd as you have the black text and then come across the red rubric text telling you where your hands should be or what you should be doing. Also, the red text is always printed in a different font and type size than the black text."

RUBRICS IN THE CLASSROOM

How did we get from Roman law and the directions for religious ceremonies to classroom assessment? When educators realized that written criteria lists provided students with the guidelines and direction for their work, the connection was obvious. Just like "Mr. Marks," the high school English teacher with my former student, we teachers always seem to be able to picture the exemplary work.

However, as Goodrich Andrade (2000) tells us, "We often expect students to just *know* what makes a good essay, a good drawing, or a good science project" (p. 15). We think that what constitutes an exemplary product must be obvious, so we don't bother to communicate all the details. However, the quality of student work often demonstrates that we need to provide more information. Developing a scoring rubric will provide the detail and direction that all students need.

At a workshop in the 1990s, the presenter, Jay McTighe of the Maryland Education Consortium, told the audience of elementary and middle school educators that students need to know what a "good one" looks like. It made sense. Or as an experienced primary teacher put it, "Students must understand the rules of the game before they can participate" (Harmon, 2001, p. 37).

Most of us can remember taking our state's driver test. We knew we were going to have to parallel park, or drive the serpentine, or drive through the local main street, and we practiced accordingly. We knew what the good driver's actions looked like; we knew the rules of the game.

Going a step further, McTighe told the teachers that students also needed to know what a "bad one" looks like. Many teachers save exemplary work to use as examples for students to model. However, few save the work that did not quite measure up. (Note of caution: Always remove all student identification to protect privacy.) As we exhibit student work and point out sets of criteria that describe levels of performance or understanding, we are, in actuality, using scoring rubrics to evaluate and measure that student work.

HISTORY OF GRADING AND STUDENT ACHIEVEMENT

When teachers evaluate or measure a student's work and assign a percentage or a letter grade, we are "grading" that work (Speck and Jones, 1998; Tchudi, 1986). But grades were not always a part of the American education scene. Prior to the 1770s, assessment and student feedback were done through narrative comments. However, in the late 1770s, Yale University began using a 4-point scale to respond to students' work, which may be the origin of the 4.0 system that is still used today.

By 1877, Harvard initiated a 6-division method of assessment, with Division 1 being a 90 percent or higher and Division 6 being below 40 percent. This was followed by Mount Holyoke College's 1897 assignment of letter grades from A to E with A being an excellent 95 or higher and E representing a failing score of below 75 (Marzano, 2000).

Grades represent an informed judgment made by a professional. However, the informed part has often meant that the grader (teacher) was informed, but the "gradee" (the student and often the parent) was not. (See box 1.1 for an analogy on grading.)

Box 1.1 Grading Analogy

Statureland is an island nation with one major industry—purple fruit. Since purple fruit picking is essential to the welfare of the whole society, the Statureland schools' basic curriculum is intended to train effective purple fruit pickers. Because purple fruit grows only at the top of 8-foot trees, the most important and critical course within the curriculum has been growing. All children are required to take growing and are expected to complete six feet of growth, which is the minimum average height of Staturelandians, based on standardized growing tests.

The course content of growing includes stretching, reaching, jumping, standing on tiptoes, and thinking tall. Each year each child's skills and abilities in growing have been assessed and each child assigned a grade.

Those children who achieved average scores on the standardized growing tests were assigned C grades. Students who, through their commitment
to growing, exceeded expected levels, received As. Slow growing students
received Fs and were regularly and publicly admonished for their lack of
effort and inattention to task. These latter children often developed poor
self-images and antisocial behavior that disrupted the school program and
interfered with children who really wanted to grow.

"This will never do," said the people. "We must call a wise man to
consider our problem and tell us how to help the children grow better and
faster and become happy purple fruit pickers." So a wise man was sent for,
and he studied the problem. At last he suggested two solutions:

1. Plant pink fruit trees that grow only five feet tall so that even students
   who are four feet tall may be successful fruit pickers.
2. Provide ladders so that all students who wish to pick purple fruit can
   reach the tips of the trees.

"No, no," said the people. "This will never work. How can we then give
grades if eight-foot trees are goals for some students and five-foot trees are
goals for other students? How can it be fair to the naturally tall students if
children on ladders can also stand six feet tall and reach the purple fruit?
However shall we give grades?"

"Ah," said the wise man, "you can't. You must decide whether you
want to grade children or have fruit picked."

Source: Adapted from L. Brisco, personal communication, April 1997, Indiana University of Pennsylvania.

An example of this lack of grading information occurred when a new
elementary principal was asked by an experienced third grade teacher to sit
in on a grade conference with a parent about a spelling grade that her son had
received on his report card. The teacher explained that the mother had the rep-
utation of causing trouble, and although she had it under control, she wanted
the principal in there just for appearances. The mother walked in armed with
the son's spelling tests for the past nine weeks. He had received an A on each
one. Why, then, had he received a B on the report card? This teacher was not
a rookie, and yet she answered, "He's just not an A speller."

The parent then asked to see the spelling grades that were recorded for her
son. All the teacher had recorded in the spelling section of her grade book
were the test scores. Again the teacher said that in comparison to other students, he was not an A speller. However, without documentation, the teacher
was headed for trouble.

At this point, the principal asked the teacher if she had any other samples of the child's work that illustrated spelling. The teacher produced a recent class assignment, and the parent was able to compare the child's work with the work of other students (once all student names were covered), and the teacher was indeed correct. He was not an A speller except on the weekly test.

The parent then posed the question, "Did he know that this work was included in his report card spelling grade?" Although the teacher assured the parent that the student was aware of this, it was clear that the parents were never informed. The veteran teacher learned several lessons that day: She needed to document and record those other grades for spelling; she needed to remind students that she was using other work to assess and grade spelling; and she needed to inform parents about her grading criteria.

Although there is controversy and debate on the effectiveness of the motivation of grades (Kohn, 1999; Marzano, 2000), research has shown that when students understand and contribute to the grading criteria, they are more enthusiastic and more actively involved in the learning process (Andrade,1997; Black, Harrison, Lee, Marshall, and Wiliam, 2004; Holmes and Smith, 2003; Jensen, 2005; Marzano, 2000). In addition, when parents understand the grading criteria, there is less need for the parent conference as described above.

LEARNING THEORIES AND USING RUBRICS

In addition to providing information on how great (and less than great) student products are, using scoring rubrics in education has other values and purposes for all students.

Learning theorists have produced a variety of philosophies on learning. These philosophies include the belief that, although students differ in learning styles and learning rates, all students are capable of learning. Other concepts include statements that learning is an individual and a social process; that students learning at all is more important than when they learn; that all students can be successful learners; that students learn best in a safe and orderly environment; and that learning is a lifelong process (Andrade, 1997; Black, Harrison, Lee, Marshall, and Wiliam, 2004; Holmes and Smith, 2003; Marzano, 2000).

There are at least 10 major theories of learning as listed in box 1.2. These theories include behaviorism, brain-based learning, brain dominance, community of practice, control theory, constructivism, developmental learning, learning styles, multiple intelligences, and social learning. All of these theories agree that for learning to occur, students must be actively participating in the process (Bandura, 1977; Dewey, 1997; Jenkins and Keefe, 2002; Perkins, 1999; Schunk, 1991; Vygotsky, 1986). Box 1.2 provides a summary of each theory, the theorist(s) associated with the theory, and the theory's connection to assessment by rubric.

Box 1.2 Learning Theories and Using Rubrics for Assessment

Constructivism (Vygotsky)

- Students construct their perspective of the world based on individual experiences and schema (i.e., mental model). The focus is on preparing the learner to problem solve in ambiguous situations.
- Instructional method: Scaffolding—the adult continually adjusts the level of help in response to the child's level of performance.
- Assessment: Assessment methods target both the level of actual development (what students can do own their own) and the zone of proximal development (what they can do with help).
- Rubric connection: Scoring and instructional rubrics provide for both levels of achievement.

Behaviorism (Skinner)

- Learning is based on behavioral changes and focuses on a new behavioral pattern being repeated until it becomes automatic.
- Instructional method: Drill and repetition.
- Assessment: Objective tests.
- Rubric connection: Rubrics can be designed to use with memorization tasks, but are not usually necessary. Rubrics can be used to help in the development of test items.

Developmental Theory (Piaget)

- Children build mental "maps" or "schema" as a basis for learning and understanding.
- Instructional method: Teachers must activate prior knowledge and help build connections with experiences.
- Assessment: Individual based on child's prior knowledge.
- Rubric connection: Rubrics provide for individuality.

Brain-Based Learning (R. Sylwester; E. Jensen)

- The biological structure and function of the brain are the basis for learning. Situations and conditions foster learning.

- Instructional method: Students must feel safe (relaxed alertness) to actively participate in the learning.
- Assessment: Opportunities exist for students to understand their own learning styles and preferences.
- Rubric connection: Student-generated rubrics reduce anxiety.

Learning Styles (D. A. Kolb)

- Abstract, concrete, active, or reflective styles.
- Instructional methods: papers and analogies (abstract learner); labs, field work, observations (concrete learner); simulations, case studies, and homework (active learner); learning logs, journals, and brainstorming (reflective learner).
- Assessment: Asks, "How are you smart?" Not "How smart are you?" A variety of assessment techniques are suggested.
- Rubric connection: Rubrics—with student input—are perfect for all four styles and can provide for a variety of criteria.

Multiple Intelligences (H. Gardner)

- There are at least seven (more are being researched) ways (intelligences) that people perceive and understand the world. The original seven are linguistic, logical/mathematical, musical, spatial, bodily-kinesthetic, interpersonal, and intrapersonal.
- Instructional method: Provide a balanced curriculum of activities that appeal to all the intelligences.
- Assessment: Takes into account the diversity of intelligences. Self-assessment tools are used.
- Rubric connection: Rubrics are supportive of student self-assessment in a variety of activities.

Right Brain/Left Brain (R. W. Sperry)

- The two different sides of the brain control two different ways of learning. Each of us prefers one mode over the other. (The right side controls the "artsy" and left is the logical.)
- Instructional method: Techniques that connect with both sides of the students' brains.
- Assessment: Provide for right-brained talents and skills (projects and portfolios) as well as the objective testing for left-brained students.

- Rubric connection: Rubrics are used to assess subjective, qualitative work.

Communities of Practice (J. Dewey and Institute for Research on Learning, Palo Alto, CA)

- Learning is social, and connecting to real-life scenarios helps students attain knowledge. No learning without doing.
- Instructional method: Hands-on methods and cooperative groups for real-life scenarios.
- Assessment: Projects and group problem solving.
- Rubric connection: Rubrics can be created for labs and other hands-on assignments, especially for cooperative group projects.

Control Theory (W. Glasser)

- Learning behavior is motivated by basic human needs: survival, love, power, freedom, and so on.
- Instructional method: Cooperative, active learning techniques that support basic needs (including power) of the learners.
- Assessment: Successful work using an absolute standard.
- Rubric connection: "Benchmarks" of scoring rubrics provide the absolute standard.

Social Learning Theory (A. Bandura)

- Based on the thought processes behind the behavior. Changes in behavior are observed, but only as an indicator as to what is occurring in the learner's brain.
- Instructional method: Social modeling.
- Assessment: Students are assessed on what they have observed and their own added creativity.
- Rubric connection: Rubrics provide the model of excellence and provide for assessment of creativity.

Source: Adapted from Bandura, 1977; Gardner, 199; Glasser, 1986; Hartman, 1995; Jensen, 2005; Kolb, 1984; Learning Theories, 2001; Quinlan, 2003; Schunk, 1991, Sylwester, 1997.

Followers of Piaget's developmental schema theory and Vygotsky's constructivist theory agree that the prior knowledge, or schema, of learners provides the basis for students to construct their own knowledge. Vygotsky professed that teachers should be coaches on the side to help students scaffold knowledge and make connections to prior knowledge. Scoring rubrics are a subtle way for students to activate prior knowledge and for teachers to assist students in acquiring new information (scaffolding).

Bandura's social cognitive theory is based on students modeling what they observe and making it their own. He pointed out that modeling was not simply imitation but that people take what they have observed and add their own creativity (Bandura, 1986). When students have a set of guidelines or model in mind (or in hand), they know exactly where they are headed (what a "good one" looks like) and can participate accordingly. Teachers, who are teaching for student achievement, are comfortable in providing a blueprint for active participation in the assignment.

Behaviorists focus on drill and repetition. Since assessment of memorized items (multiplication tables or states and capitals, for instance) can be easily assessed objectively as a percentage of items correctly memorized, rubrics are not necessary for assessing student scores by the behaviorists. However, behaviorists can use rubrics to evaluate the subjective decisions that must be made in choosing and creating questions for their objective tests (Arter and McTighe, 2001; Schunk, 1991).

Those who study the uniqueness of the brain as a basis for learning subscribe to the theories known as brain based, multiple intelligences, learning styles, and brain dominance (right brain, left brain). All four of these unique brain philosophies support the use of scoring rubrics to enhance student achievement. Again, the assessment criteria can be manipulated to accommodate the variety of students and their activities or projects and products in each classroom (Andrade, 1997; Arter and McTighe, 2001; Jensen, 2005; Schunk, 1991).

Control theory is based on the belief that the learner will learn only if motivated by the control of basic needs including power and freedom. It also proposes that absolute standards must be met. Followers of this theory know that using a scoring rubric will provide students with that absolute standard (benchmark) as well as meeting the basic needs of empowering students to provide input on their assessment and giving them the freedom of choice.

Community of practice theory is a relatively new title of what John Dewey and other progressives told educators years ago: Students learn by doing in a social environment. The subjectively assessed projects that are produced by actual doing can be difficult to grade fairly. Using scoring rubrics to assess the hands-on projects produced by cooperative groups can facilitate teacher grading. This theory reminds many of survivor-type or new talent TV shows that are based on a community of practice. Unfortunately, a detailed rubric is not provided for the participants to help them to avoid being voted off the island or hearing those dreaded words "you're going home."

If rubrics were provided, we can only imagine the scenario of the banished participant's looking back over his or her shoulder to the assessing group and demanding, "How can you do this? It wasn't even included in your rubric!"

SUMMARY

This chapter defined educational rubrics as tools to help educators establish criteria needed to make decisions to fairly evaluate and assess student work. It also provided illustrations of how we use mental rubrics in our daily lives, presented the history of rubrics and grading, offered examples of why educators use scoring rubrics, and connected rubric use to various theories of learning.

REFERENCES

All words: Rubric (2004). Retrieved January 9, 2010: www.allwords.com/wow .php?getDate=1999–08–18.

Andrade, H. G. (1997). Understanding rubrics. *Educational Leadership, 54*(4), 44–48.

Arter, J., and McTighe, J. (2001). *Scoring rubrics in the classroom: Using performance criteria for assessing and improving student performance.* Thousand Oaks, CA: Corwin Press.

Bandura, A. (1986). *Social foundations of thought and action: A social cognition theory.* Englewood Cliffs, NJ: Prentice Hall.

Bandura, A. (1977). *Social learning theory.* Englewood Cliffs, NJ: Prentice Hall.

Black, P., Harrison, C., Lee, C., Marshall, B., and Wiliam, D. (2004). Working inside the black box: Assessment for learning in the classroom. *Phi Delta Kappan, 86*(1), 9–21.

Dewey, J. (1997). *Experience and education.* New York: Simon and Shuster.

Gardner, H. (1991). Assessment in context: The alternative to standardized testing. In B. R. Gifford and M. C. O'Connor (Eds.), *Changing assessments: Alternative views of aptitude, achievement and instruction,* 239–52. Boston, MA: Kluwer.

Glasser, W. (1986). *Control theory in the classroom.* New York: Harper and Row.

Goodrich Andrade, H. (2000). Using rubrics to promote thinking and learning. *Educational Leadership,* 57(5), 13–18.

Harman, N. (2001). Student implementation of the rubric. In G. L. Taggart, S. J. Phifer, J. A. Nixon, and M. Wood (Eds.), *Rubrics: A handbook for construction and use* (pp. 37–44). Lanham, MD: Scarecrow Press.

Hartman, V. F. (1995, Summer). Teaching and learning style preferences: Transitions through technology. *VCCA Journal* 9(2), 18–20.

Hoad, T. F. (Ed.). (1993). *The concise Oxford dictionary of English etymology.* Oxford, UK: Oxford University Press.

Holmes, L. E. and Smith, L. J. (2003). Student evaluation of faculty grading systems. *Journal of Education for Business* (6), 78, 318–23.

Jenkins, J. M., and Keefe, J. W. (2002). Two schools: Two approaches to learning. *Phi Delta Kappan* 6(83), 449–56.

Jensen, E. (2005). *Teaching with the brain in mind.* Alexandria, VA: Association for Supervision and Curriculum Development.

Kohn, A. (1999). *Punished by rewards: The trouble with gold stars, incentive plans, A's, praise, and other bribes.* Boston: Houghton Mifflin.

Kolb, D. A. (1984). *Experiential learning: Experience as the source of learning and development.* Englewood Cliffs, NJ: Prentice Hall.

Marzano, R. J. (2000). *Transforming classroom grading.* Alexandria, VA: Association for Supervision and Curriculum Development.

NEA. (1993). *Student portfolios.* Washington, DC: NEA Professional Library.

Perkins, D. (1999). The many faces of constructivism. *Educational Leadership,* 57(3), 6–11.

Quinlan. A. M. (2003). *Middle level teacher certification: Does it make a difference in the perceived self-efficacy of beginning middle school teachers?* Doctoral Dissertation. Indiana: Indiana University of Pennsylvania.

Ruby aggregator and portal creator: Rubric. (2004). Retrieved January 9, 2011: rubric.rubyforge.org/#etymology.

Schunk, D. H. (1991). *Learning theories: An educational perspective.* New York: Merrill.

Speck, B. W. and Jones, T. R. (1998). Direction in the grading of writing. In F. Zak and C. Weaver (Eds.). *The theory and practice of grading writing* (pp. 17–29). Albany, NY: State University of New York Press.

Sylwester, R. (1997). The neurobiology of self-esteem and aggression. *Educational Leadership,* 54(5), 75–79.

Theories. (2001). Funderstanding. Retrieved January 17, 2011: www.funderstanding .com/theories.cfm.

Thorndike, E. L., and Barnhart, C. L. (Eds.). (1974). *Thorndike-Barnhart advanced dictionary.* Dallas, TX: Scott Foresman.

Vygotsky, L. S. (1986). *Thought and language.* Cambridge, MA: MIT Press. (Original work published 1934).

Webster's new encyclopedic dictionary. (2002). Springfield, MA: Federal Street Press.

Chapter 2

Checklists, Performance Lists, or Rubrics

Which Tool Is Right for Me?

If the only tool you have is a hammer, you tend to see every problem as a nail.

—Abraham Maslow

Rubrics are tools to help educators establish the criteria needed to make decisions in order to fairly evaluate and assess student work. However, scoring rubrics are only one tool in the teacher's assessment toolbox. Just as not all repair work requires a hammer, not all assignments require detailed scoring rubrics for assessment. A social studies quiz may not need a rubric to facilitate scoring, but if an essay question is included, a scoring rubric may be indispensable for that part of the test.

Teachers need to decide if the assignment warrants using a detailed scoring rubric, a type of checklist, or a combination of a checklist and a rubric, which is sometimes called a performance list. If a rubric is called for, the decision then becomes which type of rubric (holistic or analytic) to use. Thinking clearly about the objectives of the assignment will help teachers make these decisions.

This chapter discusses learning objectives and their relationship to developing checklists, performance lists, and rubrics. Holistic and analytic rubrics are defined, and their connection with authentic and performance-based assessment is illustrated.

DECISION 1: WHAT ARE THE OBJECTIVES OF THE ASSIGNMENT?

Objectives serve three functions for educators. First, they help teachers to identify activities and resources for effective instruction. Second, they provide the framework for evaluation, and third, they guide the teacher in directing the student. All three functions are evident in creating assessment tools. For assessment purposes, the focus is on the second and third functions of objectives, the framework for evaluation and helping to guide the learner. However, both of these functions require that teachers reflect upon the chosen activities, which is included in the first function of objectives—identifying the focus.

Objectives are usually classified as being in one of three domains: cognitive (information and knowledge), psychomotor (physical actions), or affective (attitudes). For any given task, the objectives in each of the domains should answer this question: "What do I want my students to be able to do as a result of this assignment?"

Cognitive objectives that focus on knowledge were identified and listed in a taxonomy that was created in the 1950s (Bloom, Englehart, Furst, Hill, and Krathwohl, 1956). Known as Bloom's taxonomy, this list classifies cognitive objectives by the level of thinking skills involved from simple recall, which is the lowest level objective, to the highest level of thinking skill, evaluation.

In the 1990s, educational psychologists and former students of Bloom updated the taxonomy using verbs instead of nouns. The newer terms are listed along with the originals in box 2.1. Notice that the top two levels are reversed in the newer model. However, the question to ask for objectives in the cognitive domain remains, "Do I want my students to know, comprehend, apply, analyze, synthesize, and evaluate?"

Box 2.1 Bloom's Taxonomy, General Objectives, and Verbs

Category One: Knowledge/Remembering

- Instructional objectives: Knows/remembers common terms, specific facts, methods and procedures, basic concepts, and principles.
- Verbs used in objectives: *Defines, describes, identifies, labels, locates, lists, names, states.*

Category Two: Comprehension/Understanding

- Instructional objectives: Understands facts and principles; interprets verbal materials, charts, and graphs; estimates future consequences implied in data; justifies methods and procedures.
- Verbs used in objectives: *Converts, defends, distinguishes, infers, explains, rewrites, paraphrases, gives examples, summarizes, generalizes, translates.*

Category Three: Application/Applying

* Instructional objectives: Applies concepts and principles to new situations; applies laws and theories to practical situations; demonstrates correct usage of a method or procedure.
* Verbs used in objectives: *Changes, computes, discovers, operates, manipulates, uses, modifies, predicts, produces, shows, solves, relates.*

Category Four: Analysis/Analyzing

* Instructional objectives: Recognizes unstated assumptions; recognizes logical fallacies in reasoning; distinguishes between facts and inferences; analyzes the organizational structure of a work or relevancy of data.
* Verbs used in objectives: *Breaks down, points out, differentiates, distinguishes, discriminates, relates, subdivides, surveys, outlines.*

Category Five: Synthesis/Creating *(Note that in the newer model this category is the highest or sixth level of the taxonomy.)*

* Instructional objectives: Writes a well-organized paper; gives a well-organized speech; composes a creative piece; proposes a plan or a possible solution, integrates learning from different areas into a plan for solving a problem; formulates a new scheme for classifying ideas.
* Verbs used in objectives: *Categorizes, creates, revises, rearranges, devises, combines, composes, generates, organizes, plans, reconstructs, designs.*

Category Six: Evaluation/Evaluating *(Note that in the newer model this category is the fifth level of the taxonomy.)*

* Instructional objectives: Judges the logical consistency of written material; judges the adequacy with which conclusions are supported by data; judges the value of a work using standards of excellence.
* Verbs used in objectives: *Appraises, compares, concludes, constricts, criticizes, referees, prioritizes, justifies, interprets, supports, summarizes.*

Source: Adapted from Gahagan & Jacobus, n.d.; Overbaugh & Schultz, n.d.; Morrison, Ross, & Kemp, 2004.

Educational objectives in the psychomotor domain are linked to skills of skeletal muscles, such as building something, operating a piece of equipment, or performing a physical task. The taxonomy developed by Heinich, Molenda, and Russell (1993) lists four levels of the psychomotor objectives*: imitation, manipulation, precision, and articulation.* Teachers of physical education, industrial arts, information technology, art, music, languages, and any subject that includes a lab setting write objectives in this domain. Primary teachers who focus on handwriting and the formation of letters and numerals are also working with objectives in the psychomotor domain.

Because objectives in the third domain (affective) refer to attitudes and feelings, these objectives may be the most difficult to measure and evaluate. Unless a student actually expresses an attitude—"I loved doing this" or "This was fun"—teachers are required to make inferences based on observed behaviors. These behaviors would include the amount of enthusiasm expressed, encouraging others, or even facial expression.

Although there are three distinct domains of objectives, these objectives are not mutually exclusive. One assignment may include objectives in all three domains. For example, a science teacher wants his seventh grade students to be able to list the parts of a cell as well as explain the function of each part. In recognizing this, he has just listed cognitive objectives with verbs *list* and *explain* reflecting the knowledge and comprehension areas of Bloom's taxonomy. He also wants them to have fun doing this—an objective in the affective domain.

Now that he knows what he wants his students to do, he has to decide on an activity to meet those objectives. He could simply do an objective multiple-choice or matching test, but he realizes that tests aren't fun for most students. He decides on having them create *cell songs.* He has just added another cognitive objective (create) in the synthesis area of Bloom's taxonomy.

After presenting his idea to the music teacher, he decides let them choose to work in small groups or individually to parody well-known songs with lyrics that include the cell theory and parts of the cell with their functions. He wants a written copy and an actual performance (an objective in the psychomotor domain) of the song either live or on tape. Now that the science teacher has objectives and a mental picture of what he wants his students to do, or what a good product looks like, he is ready to decide how to evaluate and score the students' work.

DECISION 2: WILL A SIMPLE CHECKLIST OR AN EXPANDED CHECKLIST DO?

Checklists are simple tools that usually list the components that must be present in a student product. Usually no scoring or value is involved since the item can be checked as either present or not present. Technically no other criteria are used; there is no judgment of quality. The item is either there or not there.

Checklists are for objectives in all three domains: cognitive, psychomotor, and affective. A cognitive checklist of the parts of a friendly letter would indicate that the student is able to identify the date, greeting, body, closing, and signature of a friendly letter. A psychomotor checklist may include physical skills, such as the ability to dribble a basketball or jog three times around the gym.

A combination *cognitive/psychomotor* checklist for a student-created graph may include components that the student was required to include such as *title, labeling on axes, legend, scale, and data points. Affective* checklists may consist of verbs such as *volunteers, joins in, cooperates, enjoys.*

Examples of simple checklists used to clarify a playground conflict or to audit the literacy emphasis of a classroom are shown below.

PLAYGROUND CONFLICT CHECKLIST (to be attached to a report)

LEVELS OF STUDENTS INVOLVED:

———— primary

———— intermediate

———— middle school

GENDER:

———— male

———— female

NATURE OF CONFLICT:

———— verbal

———— physical

ACTIVITY PRECEDING CONFLICT:

———— game (football, basketball, keep away, other:_____)

———— unknown

OTHER INFORMATION: (optional) _____

CHECKLIST FOR A LITERACY-CENTERED CLASSROOM

Place a checkmark if the item is present.

———— 1. An area is present where students can find books and other materials for independent reading.

———— 2. An area is present where students can find materials for writing and book making.

———— 3. Student writing is available for other students to read.

———— 4. Student work is displayed in the classroom.

———— 5. A listening area is available where students can listen to a favorite story.

———— 6. Procedures are in place for students to regularly share with their classmates—writing a puppet play, an explanation of a project that has been completed.

———— 7. There are materials appropriate to all ability levels in the reading, writing, and listening areas.

———— 8. If a visitor walks into the room, there is evidence that reading, writing, and oral language are being promoted/encouraged/facilitated.

———— 9. All students spend 10–15 minutes per day engaged in silent reading.

———— 10. Students are read aloud to each day.

———— 11. All students spend 10–15 minutes per day writing.

———— 12. There are occasions for students to share a favorite book and author.

———— 13. Communication takes place with parents to inform them of the classroom environment and the important role they can play in extending reading, writing, and responding at home.

———— 14. Reading and writing links are made across the curriculum.

EXPANDED CHECKLIST

If some type of evaluation or judgment is needed, but the teacher does not have to assign a numerical score, then an *expanded checklist* is used. An expanded checklist provides the opportunity for simple evaluation of the criteria present.

Elementary language arts teachers often use expanded checklists to organize information gleaned from observations of students' accomplishments in reading and writing over time. These dated lists often use a simple code of a checkmark if the item is present, a zero if it is not observed, or a plus sign to indicate that the behavior is consistently present. For example, if a teacher is assessing the word identification strategies that students use when they come upon unfamiliar words, the categories on the checklist may be

- Uses syllables to decode
- Continues reading to use context clues
- Uses pictures to glean meaning
- Substitutes an acceptable word
- Refers to prior experience with the word

Teachers may use a check, a plus, or a zero when assessing these strategies. A checkmark may indicate that the child attempted to employ the strategy, a plus may indicate that the child used the strategy successfully, and a zero would indicate that this strategy was not used. If teachers are using the checkmark, plus sign, and zero to assess these skills, they have the foundation to convert this list to a scoring rubric if needed. An example of this type of assessment is below:

SAMPLE EXPANDED CHECKLIST

Writing Checklist

Emergent Literacy—Writing Process

Student _____ Date _____ Grade_____
Teacher_____

Grading Code:

+ = consistently present

0 = not present

✓ = sometimes present/needs instruction

General Writing Behaviors

_____ Enjoys writing

_____ Is confident about writing

_____ Writes spontaneously

_____ Reads others' writing

_____ Writes in a variety of formats

Mechanics and Conventions

_____ Forms letters conventionally

_____ Shows increased phonemic awareness

_____ Uses invented spelling and edits

_____ Is learning spelling families and patterns

_____ Recognizes errors and edits own writing

_____ Uses word processing

Writing Process

_____ Participates in stages of writing process

_____ Writes both collaboratively and independently

_____ Reacts to others' writing

(Cooper and Kiger, 2005; Tompkins, 2010).

Although some rubric purists disdain the use of checklists, these listings can serve as a strong foundation for developing in-depth performance lists and eventually creating scoring rubrics. For example, each item on the graph checklist or the parts of a letter checklist can be expanded to include detailed criteria for scoring.

The science teacher with the cell song assignment can quickly list the components of the assignment: cell theory, cell parts and their functions, must be a song, written copy, performance. These items could simply be checked off on a checklist, but his seventh graders want to know if this is for a grade. A simple checklist won't help with the grading, and an expanded checklist will not give the numerical score needed for a grade. Perhaps he can use a performance list.

DECISION 3: WILL A PERFORMANCE LIST DO?

If your objective is to have students come to class with a pencil, notebook, and textbook, or to have them identify the components of a graph, then a checklist is appropriate. If you need to assign a grade or numerical score to student work, then you may want to consider creating a performance list. A *performance list*, also known as an assessment list, is a list of items to rate along with a rating scale.

A simple performance list is a combination of a checklist with more in-depth evaluation. Usually it has the possible number of points listed and a space for the points or "score" assigned by the evaluator.

The science teacher who was having students create cell songs was required to grade work on a scale that was 93–100 for an A; 85–92 for a B; and so on, so he decided that this would be a 100-point project and created the performance list that is illustrated in below.

Since he was required to grade work on a scale that was 93–100 for an A; 85–92 for a B; and so on, so he decided that this would be a 100-point project and created the performance list that is illustrated below.

SAMPLE PERFORMANCE LIST

Cell Song Performance List

100 points possible

Students: _____

10 Cell Components—Possible 70 points
Components mentioned in song (2 points each)
Function described or explained in song (5 points each)

_____ Cell theory

Organelles:

_____ Cell membrane

_____ Cell wall (plants only)

_____ Nucleus

_____ Vacuole

_____ Chloroplast (plants only)

_____ Endoplasmic reticulum

_____ Ribosome

_____ Mitochondria

_____ Golgi apparatus

Other components—30 points

_____ Recognizable tune (possible 5 points)

_____ Written lyrics—neatly done and spelled correctly (possible 15 points)

_____ Performed live or taped (possible 10 points)

Total _____

Comments:

As the teacher evaluated each song, he quickly awarded 2 points for the mention of a cell part. If he found the correct mention of the function of that part, he added 5 more points. Note that spelling and neatness were worth 15 points, which gave the teacher a wider range of points to award in this area. Since his students had a copy of this performance list, they knew the criteria for the work and were not surprised by any additions.

Performance lists help teachers to grade subjective projects and portfolios by providing a guide for evaluation. Making a copy of the performance list for each student and using that copy when grading the project can facilitate the assessment procedure.

By providing a range of points for each item, the performance list maintains the teacher's professional judgment for each category. That is, the teacher may award 5 points or 1 point for neatness depending on expectations. Performance lists are great for assigning numerical scores (points earned), but they often do not have the precise criteria of each listed area, so some students are left wondering.

Once teachers have decided that the assessment is more than a case of the item simply being present or not, the assessment has moved from a checklist to the category of a performance list. And the performance list may be all that is needed for evaluation. However, if you need to justify each grade or would like your students to consistently produce quality projects, then you may want to take the next step to developing a scoring rubric by adding precise criteria to each item on your list.

DECISIONS 4 AND 5: IS A DETAILED SCORING RUBRIC NEEDED, AND IF SO, WHAT KIND?

The rubric is a tool to help educators establish criteria needed to make decisions to fairly evaluate and assess student work. Although the performance list is a great start to a fair evaluation, it does not usually clearly define the criteria that the evaluator may have in mind. If teachers would like their students to reliably create quality projects and thoroughly understand each scoring point, they may want to take the next step from performance list to scoring rubric.

There are five advantages of using precise sets of criteria that describe levels of performance or understanding in a scoring rubric:

- Rubrics provide students with expectations about what will be assessed.
- Rubrics provide students with information on the standards that need to be met.
- Rubrics provide students with indications of where they are in relation to goals.
- Rubrics increase consistency in teacher ratings of performance, products, or understanding.
- Rubrics provide teachers with data to support grades.

If the science teacher wanted to describe the criteria or expectations of each component of the cell song assignment, wanted to make sure each song was graded on the same criteria, and was comfortable using a 0–4 grading scale, then a scoring rubric may have been his best bet. The primary reading teacher with the checklist on word identification strategies may want to add details that indicate if the student needed to be prompted to use the strategy or was able to use the strategy independently. Both of these scenarios would warrant using a scoring rubric.

Experts in the world of rubrics divide rubrics into two main categories: *holistic* and *analytic*, which is a logical dichotomy depending on the purpose of the teacher and the objectives of the assignment. As the name implies, a holistic rubric evaluates the entire project and yields one numerical score (usually between 0 and 4 or 0 and 6). The rubric in box 2.2 illustrates sample 4-point and 6-point holistic rubrics. In the 4-point rubric, the 4 points are earned for exemplary work—beyond expectations; the 3 points are for good, solid-quality work (the benchmark); and the 2 and 1 are awarded for those projects that are lacking in some respects. Note that the zero is reserved for the student who does not turn in anything at all.

A word of caution is required when writing description terms for rubrics. A well-know educator uses the descriptor "rarely or never" for a score of one point on a 4-point rubric. The question remains, if students *never* exhibit the trait, how do they earn a point? ALWAYS include a "zero" on rubrics for work not submitted.

Box 2.2 Sample 4-Point and 6-Point Holistic Rubrics

Generic 4-POINT HOLISTICRUBRIC

4. Advanced (in-depth understanding)—Exemplary performance or understanding; shows creativity.
3. Proficient (general understanding)—Solid performance or understanding; the *standard*.
2. Basic (partial understanding)—Performance/understanding is emerging or developing; makes errors; has a grasp that is not thorough.
1. Below basic (minimal understanding)—Might attempt but has serious errors or misconceptions.
0. No attempt made.

Generic 6-POINT HOLISTIC RUBRIC

6. Exemplary achievement—Detailed understanding with creativity or originality.

5. Commendable achievement—Detailed understanding; the *standard*.
4. Adequate achievement—General understanding.
3. Some evidence of achievement—Partial understanding.
2. Limited evidence of achievement—Little understanding.
1. Minimal evidence of achievement—No understanding.
0. No response

The 6-point holistic rubric above can also be used as a template from which to build specific subject-related rubrics. Scores 6 and 5 would be considered high with 5 being the standard or benchmark, scores 4 and 3 would be high-average and low-average respectively, and scores 2 and 1 would be for attempts that need revision. The exact behavior that is to be evaluated would be briefly described under each number. Again, the 0 is reserved for students not attempting the assignment.

A holistic rubric is used when teachers want to evaluate the entire product or performance based on their overall impression of the work. The critical components are listed as the benchmark items under item 3 in a 4-point rubric, or under item 5 in a 6-point rubric. For example, if using a holistic rubric to evaluate a student's assignment to deliver a persuasive speech, the critical components may be volume, clarity, grammar, and content. A possible holistic rubric for this is illustrated in box 2.3 below. The student would earn one of five possible scores, 4, 3, 2, 1, or 0.

Box 2.3 Holistic Rubric for Persuasive Speech

Persuasive Speech Rubric

4 Points (Exemplary)
  Volume—loud enough for all to hear
  Clarity—extremely articulate and easy to understand
  Grammar—no grammatical errors
  Content—convinces the audience and entertains or holds interest

3 Points (benchmark)
  Volume—loud enough for most to hear
  Clarity—articulate and easy to understand
  Grammar—1–3 grammatical errors
  Content—convinces the audience

2 Points
   Volume—audible only to audience members closest to speaker
   Clarity—difficult to understand
   Grammar—more than 3 grammatical errors
   Content—convinces some of the audience

1 Point
   Volume—all have difficulty in hearing
   Clarity—mumbles
   Grammar—excessive grammatical errors
   Content—no one is convinced; weak argument

0 Points
   Does not attempt

Source: Adapted with permission: L. Hoffmann, teacher, Norwin Middle School, N. Huntingdon, PA (personal communication, November 3, 2005).

In comparison, the analytic rubric actually dissects the project and provides a separate score for each item or component. There is no set requirement for the number of traits to incorporate in an analytic rubric. Once again, the evaluator should feel free to include all traits deemed necessary for evaluation. Often, the complexity or simplicity of the task will determine the number of traits to include for assessment.

An analytic rubric of the same persuasive speech assignment may look like the rubric in box 2.4. Each component—volume, clarity, grammar, and content—is scored independently, and the scores are totaled for each area. Some educators use an average score for the product by dividing the total points by the number of criteria, and others simply record the total points earned. Again, a zero is reserved for the student who does not even attempt the assignment. (Chapter 12 deals with converting the rubric score to real-world grades.)

Box 2.4 Analytic Rubric for Persuasive Speech

Volume

4. Loud enough for all to hear; uses volume effectively to make points and get attention.
3. Loud enough for all to hear (benchmark).

2. Loud enough for most to hear.
1. Audible only to audience members closest to speaker.
0. Did not participate. Unable to evaluate.

Clarity of Speaking

4. Extremely articulate and easy to understand.
3. Articulate and easy to understand (benchmark).
2. Difficult to understand.
1. Mumbles.
0. Did not participate. Unable to evaluate.

Grammar

4. No grammatical or usage errors.
3. Fewer than three grammatical or usage errors (benchmark).
2. More than three grammatical or usage errors.
1. So many errors that it hurts to listen.
0. Did not participate. Unable to evaluate.

Content

4. Convinces the audience and entertains; holds interest.
3. Convinces the audience; strong argument (benchmark).
2. Convinces some of the audience.
1. Very few or no one convinced; weak argument.
0. Did not participate. Unable to evaluate.

Total score _____

Source: Adapted with permission: L. Hoffmann, teacher, Norwin Middle School, N. Huntingdon, PA. (personal communication, May 14, 2011).

There are advantages and disadvantages to both holistic and analytic rubrics. The holistic rubric is simpler and more efficient. It is often used to judge a simple product with an overall score. Because of the relative simplicity of the holistic rubric, teachers wanting to create scoring rubrics usually begin with this type. Another advantage of a holistic rubric is that a large number of student responses can be evaluated quickly. Holistic rubrics are often used in large-scale assessments at the state or national levels and have become more common as states fall in line with the requirements of No Child Left Behind.

A disadvantage of using holistic rubrics is that few details are provided in the analysis. Two students who each receive a 2 on their persuasive speeches may not ever know what made them a 2. And indeed, those scores could represent totally different reasons. For example, one student may have not been loud enough while the other may have not had a very convincing argument. This lack of detailed feedback is often listed as a weakness of the holistic rubric. However, placing a section for teacher comments on the bottom of the score sheet is a way to compensate for this weakness.

In comparison, an analytic rubric provides a more detailed analysis of the performance. Students can ascertain where their strengths and weaknesses lie. Another advantage of the analytical rubric is that teachers have the ability to weight the scores of a trait they want to emphasize. For example, if content is more important than performance in the persuasive speech, the content may be weighted at 50 percent of the persuasive speech score, while the remaining weight can be divided among the other criteria deemed less critical at that time.

AUTHENTIC ASSESSMENT, PERFORMANCE-BASED ASSESSMENT, AND RUBRICS

Two terms often associate with the use of scoring rubrics in education are authentic and performance-based assessments. Assessment usually refers to the gathering of data or information about a student's performance; assigning a score or grade to that data is the evaluation. The term *authentic assessment*, when used in an educational format, indicates that the tasks, products, or performances are like actual products and performances in the "real world." Performance-based assessment means that the data are based on the student's actions or performance in a real-world scenario, not simply on a multiple-choice test.

Scoring an authentic task is more difficult than scoring an objective test. Because rubrics provide a numerical or quantitative way of evaluating a qualitative assignment, they can help to ease some of the difficulty in evaluating, or scoring, authentic or performance-based tasks. In addition, using assessment tools, such as performance lists or detailed scoring rubrics, can actuallyincrease student and teacher learning.

Since these tools provide information that both teachers and students can use as feedback, the lists and rubrics become a component for assessing the activity as well as assessing student performance. Checklists, performance lists, and scoring rubrics are valuable tools in the teacher's assessment toolbox; you simply have to decide which tool is right for you.

Chapter 2

SUMMARY

This chapter provided background information on learning objectives as the first step in assessment decisions. Types of checklists and performance lists and their relationship to developing detailed scoring rubrics were discussed. Sample generic 4-point and 6-point rubrics were provided. Holistic and analytic rubrics were defined, and their connections with authentic and performance-based assessments were illustrated.

REFERENCES

Bloom, B. S., Englehart, M. D., Furst, E. J., Hill, W. H., and Krathwohl, D. R. (1956). *A taxonomy of educational objectives: Handbook I. The cognitive domain.*New York: McKay.

Cooper, J. D., and Kiger, N. D. (2005). *Literacy assessment: Helping teachers plan assessment* (2nd ed.). Boston: Houghton Mifflin.

Gahagan, B., and Jacobus, G. (n.d.). *Strategies! For the classroom.*Columbia, SC: Gahagan Jacobus.

Heinich, R., Molenda, M., and Russell, J. D. (1993). *Instructional media and the new technologies of instruction* (4th ed.). New York: Macmillan.

Morrison, G. R., Ross, S. M., and Kemp, J. E. (2004). *Designing effective instruction.* Edison, NJ: John Wiley and Sons.

Overbaugh, L. C. and Schultz, L. (n.d.). Bloom's taxonomy. Retrieved February 24, 2011 from www.odu.edu/educ/roverbau/Bloom/blooms_taxonomy.htm.

Tompkins, G. (2010). *Literacy for the 21st century* (5th ed.) Upper Saddle River, NJ: Merrill Prentice Hall.

Chapter 3

Using Rubrics in Primary Grades

> Give me the children until they are seven and anyone may have them afterward.
>
> —St. Francis Xavier

The primary or early childhood levels are traditionally defined as extending from kindergarten through third grade. Research has shown that these formative years, usually from ages 5 to 8, are crucial for providing a foundation for students' future success in school. Added to the mix is the federal mandate for accountability through assessment. This chapter presents discussions of primary grade curricular requirements based on developmental characteristics of children in grades K–3 and the role scoring rubrics play in the primary grades to facilitate assessment.

KINDERGARTEN AND FIRST GRADE

Kindergarten, which is German for "children's garden," was created in 1837 by Friedrich Froebel, a German educator, who believed that young children learn best by play and interaction. And although this philosophy has remained constant, the implementation of play and interaction has changed.

Walk into any kindergarten today and you may see students reading about the day's activities from a large chart, identifying sounds that letters make, creating double-digit numbers with counters bundled into tens and writing the corresponding numerals, and even figuring out why some items float and others do not. It has been well documented that students in today's kindergartens are more immersed in academic work than their parents and grandparents ever were.

Kindergarten teachers, who once spent their instructional time singing happy songs and supervising peg-board play and rhythm bands, are now incorporating language experience charts, phonemic awareness, manuscript handwriting, math, and science activities into their day. For many, kindergarten—once a half-day experience—is now an entire school day in order to facilitate all the requirements of the curriculum. And in some schools, that all-day kindergarten does not even include the traditional naptime.

This maturing of the kindergarten has had a domino effect in our primary or K–3 curricula. A teacher reminiscing about her first grade student-teaching experience in the late 1960s recalled, "There were no public kindergartens and no *Sesame Street*. We started with, 'This is an A.' Now they come to us with the expectations of an entire list of emergent literacy behaviors." A checklist of emergent literacy behaviors is illustrated below:

CHECKLIST OF EMERGENT LITERACY BEHAVIORS

1. _____ Demonstrates ability to understand oral messages

   Listens

   Responds appropriately

2. _____ Pretends to read

3. _____ Uses drawings and "writing" to communicate

   Can "read" what they wrote

4. _____ Tracks print by pointing to words

   Left to right—Top to bottom

5. _____ Can identify the jargon associate with reading

   First word in a sentence, one letter, etc.

6. _____ Recognizes familiar words in the environment (names, signs, etc.)

7. _____ Recognizes rhymes and can "play along" and add rhymes

8. _____ Names letters and matches words with same beginning sound (phonemic and phonological awareness)

9. _____ Makes the connection among print, spoken words, and concepts

10. _____ Gains awareness of the personal process of interacting with print (Allington and Walmsley, 1994; Jalongo, 2003; Tompkins, 2010).

First grade teachers know that they are responsible for the bulk of phonemic awareness skills that children need to learn. With 85 percent of all words following some phonemic or sound pattern, it's up to the first grade teachers to get their students knowledgeable about the majority of these patterns. Primary classroom teachers across the country, as well as state and local school districts feeling the pressures of complying with federal mandates, seem to be injecting academic content into every waking moment of their students' lives.

Although the mandated testing from the federal government does not begin until third grade, educators know that the foundation formed in the kindergarten and first grade classrooms is critical to those third grade scores. Research has shown that the students who do well on a first grade reading test continue that testing success through later grades. However, students who do poorly on the first grade assessment also have difficulty with testing in the upper levels. With the belief that the best predictor of future behavior is past behavior, educators have shifted a major focus on the academic curriculum of the primary grades.

Perceptive kindergarten and first grade teachers are aware that the successful way to reach their students is through structured exploration. This means providing a schedule with time for carefully constructive activities. Providing a variety of learning centers with corresponding rubrics and checklists (as illustrated in box 3.1) is well worth the time and effort for the academically centered kindergarten.

Box 3.1 Rubric for Kindergarten Measurement Center

Measurement Center

Name_____Date_____

3 = almost always

2 = sometimes

1 = not yet

———— Able to measure with nonstandard items (blocks, pennies, paper clips)

———— Able to use a ruler correctly

———— Able to use correct measurement words (inch, foot)

———— Able to complete activities at center

———— Works independently

Teacher's Comments:

Source: Adapted with permission: K. Fierle, Seton Hill Kindergarten, Greensburg, Pennsylvania.

SECOND AND THIRD GRADES

Second grade was once a time for students to strengthen all the skills learned in first grade. This "consolidation" year was best known for the student transition from manuscript writing (printing) to cursive writing and an introduction to multiplication with the two tables. A tour of second grade classrooms today will reveal posters of math vocabulary such as symmetry, vertices, and angles; examples of similes and metaphors; and even purposes for writing such as persuasive, informative, or entertaining. Principals know that the pressure is on for second graders and their teachers.

If the pressure is on in second grade, it is actually blowing the lid off in third. As required by federal law that took effect in 2002, all children in public schools take their first federally mandated standardized test in third grade. Schools risk sanctions if there is no academic improvement among enough children. A glimpse of a South Carolina school's third grade curriculum reveals that third grade students are expected to

- Write descriptive paragraphs, stories, letters, simple explanations, and short stories across all content areas
- Write letters, advertisements, notes, reminders, directions, signs, and warnings that relate to real issues at school or in the community
- Publish a variety of texts, such as stories, poems, plays, directories, newspapers, charts, diagrams, book responses, and directions appropriate for audiences

In numbers and operations, these same third graders must be able to

- Recall multiplication and division facts through the 12 table
- Apply the commutative, identity, and zero property for addition and multiplication
- Find the missing factor, divisor, or dividend in a multiplication or division sentence
- Solve problems involving the sum or difference of two whole numbers, each with five digits or less, with and without regrouping
- Use oral and written communication to explain ways of solving a problem
- Use estimation to predict results and evaluate reasonableness of those results
- Add and subtract fractions having denominators of 10 or less
- Add and subtract decimals
- Estimate the sum or difference of whole numbers having at least five digits
- Estimate the products of whole numbers up to two digits by one digit
- Use concrete models to find the sum or difference of two like fractions or decimals

- Provide real-world examples that require multiplying amounts of money
- Choose appropriate operations/symbols to illustrate and solve a variety of problems (Nelson Elementary School, 2004)

These are only 2 of the 23 curricular areas listed for the third grade where, in many states, the stakes attached to standardized tests are critical, and not making the grade on the test can result in the student repeating the grade and teachers facing salary cuts or unemployment.

DEVELOPMENTAL CHARACTERISTICS OF PRIMARY STUDENTS

In the early 1900s, John Dewey and other progressives of the times believed that children should not be pushed to read or write before the age of eight (Dewey, 1956, orig. 1902). However, in some school districts, superintendents now boast that their first graders are spending a total of one hour daily in writing activities and even more time in phonics and reading.

In the late 1980s, the term *developmentally appropriate practices* or DAP became the buzzwords for educators. Developmental needs became the basis for every choice that teachers made in their classrooms. These choices often included everything from decisions about classroom organization, curriculum, and scheduling to, of course, assessment.

To encourage positive and successful attitudes toward assessment in these critical early years, and to respond to the cry for accountability, many primary teachers find themselves spending more time than ever before in assessing student work. In discussing the assessment of these primary students from grades K–3, attention must be given to the developmental characteristics of children at these levels. Box 3.2 summarizes the typical cognitive, social, and physical developmental areas of children from ages 5 to age 8.

Box 3.2 Developmental Characteristics of Primary Students

Cognitive Development

Age 5

- Repetitive behavior maximizes learning—repeat stories, poems, songs, games, sometimes with minor variations; patterning in math, science, and daily scheduling important.

- May become stuck in repetitive behavior for fear of making a mistake when trying something new.
- Learn best through active exploration of concrete materials—blocks, manipulatives, arts and crafts, sand and water, etc.
- Seldom able to see things from another's point of view.

Age 6

- Loves to ask questions.
- Learns best through discovery.
- Enjoys process more than product.
- Cooperative play elaborated.
- Representative symbols more important.
- Spatial relationships and functional relationships better understood.

Age 7

- Likes to review learning.
- Needs closure; must complete assignments.
- Likes to work slowly and alone.
- Reflective ability growing.
- Erases constantly, wants perfection.
- Enjoys manipulatives.

Age 8

- Engrossed in activity at hand; loves to socialize at the same time.
- Often works quickly.
- Concrete operations solidifying.
- Begins to feel a sense of competence with skills.
- Interest in process and product of school work; peers' assessment of work as important as teacher's.
- Growing interest in rules, logic; keen interest in how things are put together, how they work; interest in classification.

Social Development

Age 5

- Cooperative.
- Can work at quiet activities for about 15 minutes.
- Able to pace themselves during tasks.

- Consistent planning provides security.
- Thinks aloud and then does what has been spoken.

Age 6

- School replaces home as most significant environment influence.
- Wants to be first.
- Competitive and enthusiastic.
- Sometimes a "poor sport" or cheats; invents rules.
- Failure is hard; thrives on praise.

Age 7

- Changeable feelings.
- Relies on teacher for help.
- Doesn't like to make mistakes or risk making them.
- Sensitive to others' feelings but sometimes tattles.
- Conscientious; serious.

Age 8

- Gregarious; humorous.
- Likes cooperative work.
- Often overestimates abilities.
- Resilient; bounces back quickly from mistakes.

Physical Development

Age 5

- Pincer grasp with pencil.
- Reversals common.
- Restless; tires easily.
- Falls out of chair sideways.
- Often stands to do work.
- Fine motor skills are awkward.

Age 6

- Oral activity (chews pencils, etc.).
- Visually ready for reading.
- Learning left from right.

- Noisy in classroom.
- Sloppy; in a hurry.
- Falls out of chair backwards.
- Distinguishing left from right.

Age 7

- Often works with head down on desk.
- Pincer grasp at pencil point.
- Written work tidy, neat.
- Sometimes tense.
- Likes confined space.
- Many hurts, real and imagined.

Age 8

- Somewhat awkward.
- Speedy, works in a hurry.
- Full of energy.
- Needs physical release, outdoor time.

Source: Adapted from CUIP, 2011; Grapevine-Colleyville Independent School District, 2002; PBS
   Parents, 2011; Wood, 1997.

As children enter second and third grades, they have become very knowledgeable about the expectations of the school environment. These children
question, reason, and compare and contrast.

At a school where the students are required to wipe off the lunch tables in
preparation for the next class, a second grader approached the principal with,
"Mrs. Martin, I don't have to do this at home. Why do I have to do it here?"
In addition to questioning and reasoning, they often strive for perfection. It
is not unusual to see second graders' work with repeated erasures as they
attempt to reach a flawless paper. Teachers can build upon this characteristic
by introducing self-assessment rubrics at this level.

USING SELF-ASSESSMENT RUBRICS
WITH PRIMARY STUDENTS

Because 7-year-olds can describe perfect behaviors, first and second grades
are a good time to explain self-assessment rubrics. One primary teacher
introduces a 4-point scoring rubric by using something familiar to all

students—drawing a flower scene. She begins by dividing a poster board into four parts. In the first part she draws only a circle and labels it 1. She asks her class if the drawing of a flower is complete. When they respond "no," she moves to the second n square, draws another circle, adds a line to represent a stem, and labels it with a 2. The students are again aware that more is needed for it to be a flower.

In the third square, the teacher adds leaves and petals to make a daisy-like flower. Many children now declare that the picture is complete, but she cautions them to wait until they have seen her "best effort." She then completes square number 4 with background filling in all the white area with many colors (Harmon, 2001).

Because she has shown her students what a good one looks like, this teacher can keep this poster as a display for student and even parent reference. In addition, she can build upon this flower rubric to demonstrate other academic areas from handwriting to math problems. Another early childhood teacher's classroom has on display a model 4-point manuscript handwriting rubric. Again, the 4 areas of a poster show teacher-created examples of what is and what is not acceptable in handwriting for that class. Interestingly, the 1-, 2-, and 3-point areas show individual letters, but the 4-point has a complete sentence—as decided by the class.

A group of second graders in a South Carolina school dictated the behavior rubric in box 3.3. We can tell immediately that sitting posture is a real issue in this classroom as is the amount of social interaction permitted. However, we can also determine that these students have "rubric smarts" and are probably able to self-assess other areas.

Box 3.3 Second Grade Student-Developed Rubric for Classroom Behavior

4. Don't talk. Sits on chair and lissens [sic] to teacher. Works hard. Good.
3. Talks a little. Sits on chair and mostly lissens [sic] to teacher. Works. Pretty good.
2. Talks a lot. Sits on knees and maybe lissens [sic]. Works a little bit. Bad.
1. They talk loud and never lissens [sic]. Walk all around. Don't write a thang [sic]. Bad to the bone!

Source: McTighe, J., North Allegheny Curriculum Conference, Pittsburgh, PA (personal communication, March 1996).

Can improving self-assessment raise standards? Research done in 1998 provided evidence that self-assessment techniques including scoring rubrics have a direct effect on raising standards. Students who are able to connect their work to a goal or target (as delineated on a rubric) consistently score higher on standardized tests. When students continue to self-assess, they exhibit control over their work and begin to develop the ability to think at a metacognitive level (Black, Harrison, Lee, Marshall, and Wiliam, 2004).

The process of self-assessment requires a certain amount of detachment on the part of the student. This is not always easy to teach. However, some primary teachers have had success in helping their students to learn the process through the "traffic light" method (Black, et al., 2004). By comparing the level of understanding to the red, yellow, and green of traffic lights, students can begin to assess their own understanding of academic content.

If students feel that they have a good understanding and that they can move on, they label their work with a green sticker (or draw a green circle) on the page. If students feel that they have partial understanding, they place a yellow sticker or yellow drawing on the concept. A red sticker or drawing may indicate that they are "stopped" and need to have the concept taught again.

Other teachers have students self-assess by doing thumbs-up, sideways, or down or by drawing happy faces, frowning faces, or simply a face with a straight line for the mouth. Box 3.4 has a description of a smiley face rubric used to assess writing in kindergarten and first grade in a local school. The complete face with eyes, nose, and mouth is reserved for the best work. The classic smiley face with no nose is the next level. A face with eyes only represents work that is missing key components, and the empty face suggests that little or no attempt was made.

Box 3.4 Happy Face Writing Rubric for Kindergarten and First Grade

- Complete happy face with eyes nose and mouth (highest score):
  - o Kindergarten: Complete work, very neat, has everything it needs.
  - o Beginning of first grade: One complete sentence with spacing.
  - o End of first grade: Two or more complete sentences with spacing, capital letters, and punctuation.

- Face with eyes and mouth only:
  - o Kindergarten: Almost complete work, neat, but missing a few things.
  - o Beginning of first grade: Incomplete sentence. Some spacing.
  - o End of first grade: One complete sentence. Missing some punctuation.

- Face with eyes only:
  - o Kindergarten: Not complete work. Messy, missing many things.
  - o Beginning of first grade: Illegible, no word distinction, no meaning.
  - o End of first grade: Incomplete sentences. No punctuation.

- Empty circle:
  - o Kindergarten: Missing everything or failed to attempt.
  - o Beginning of first grade: Missing everything.
  - o End of first grade: Missing everything.

Source: Adapted with permission: K. Fierle, Seton Hill Kindergarten, Greensburg, Pennsylvania (personal communication, November 30, 2004).

After students have assessed their own understanding, teachers require students to meet with others of their same level. In these peer groups, students compare and support their judgments. These discussions can provide the beginning steps for connecting self-assessment to peer assessment. Once again, teacher modeling is vital to student success with these methods.

Two different scoring rubrics used in primary math classes are listed below. The four-point primary math rubric, used in a conceptual math class in the early grades, is a tool for both teachers and students. The score of four as "got all" is easily understood. As one second grade teacher said, "*All* means *all*, and my students know that's what it means. They need to get the answer and the explanation."

FOUR-POINT PRIMARY MATH SCORING RUBRIC

4. Got all. No mistakes.
3. Got most. Minor mistakes that are easily corrected with a clue from the teacher.
2. Got some. Many mistakes.
1. Got a little. Attempted, but re-teaching is required.
0. Did not attempt.

Students who earn threes—"got most"—make minor mistakes that are easily corrected with a clue from the teacher. For example, in doing a money problem, the student omitted the dollar sign in the answer. When the teacher asks, "How will I know that answer is money?" the student quickly adds a dollar sign and decimal point. If students make mistakes in computation, the teacher may only need to ask if they are sure of their answer to get an immediate correction for the 3 points.

Students on the right track but who have more complex errors earn the 2. The student who attempts the problem and starts to write down the numbers but is stumped beyond that point is an example of a 1. And, as in all rubrics, the zero is reserved for the student who fails to attempt the assignment.

The kindergarten math rubric below has scoring guide descriptors to help parents understand scoring methods. It also leaves spaces for teacher comments. It is used at the completion of a unit or as a progress report to parents. The teachers using this rubric find the format is easily adapted to a variety of concepts for areas other than math.

KINDERGARTEN MATH RUBRIC

Scoring guide:

4. *Outstanding Performance* (Completes task without assistance. Uses verbal skills effectively. Demonstrates flexibility in thinking.)
3. *Competent Performance* (Completes task with minimal assistance. Demonstrates understanding of concept.)
2. *Passive Performance* (Needs frequent help to complete task. Needs more time to understand concept.)
1. *Weak Performance/Re-teach* (Does not demonstrate adequate understanding of the concept.)

Concepts Assessed with Teacher Observation Score

   Recognizes Numbers ———

   Counts and Sorts Objects ———

   Makes Patterns and Sequences ———

   Uses Manipulatives to Solve Problems ———

   Talks about the Task and Describes Thought Process to Teacher ———

   Estimates Answers ———

   Writes Numbers ———

Used with permission: K. Fierle, Seton Hill Kindergarten, Greensburg, Pennsylvania (personal communication, May 14, 2011).

SUMMARY

Using rubrics in the primary grades can provide a foundation for understanding the focus of assessment. Students who become comfortable with various rubrics to score their work in the early grades are better able to self-assess and review and revise work in the later grades. In addition, rubrics provide documentation for celebrating progress. As a pre-service teacher observing a third grade noted, "They get so happy when they do well."

This chapter provided information on the primary grades curriculum and how it connects to the developmental characteristics of children in grades K–3. Examples of scoring rubrics appropriate for use in the early grades were provided.

REFERENCES

Allington, R., and Walmsley, S. (1994). *No quick fix*. Newark, DE: International Reading Association.

Black, P., Harrison, C., Lee, C., Marshall, B., and Wiliam, D. (2004). Working inside the black box: Assessment for learning in the classroom. *Phi Delta Kappan, 86*(1), 9–21.

CUIP (2011). Developmental characteristics and interests of school-age children. Retrieved may 5, 2011 from cuip.uchicago.edu/~cac/nlu/tie512win10/articles/developmental%20characteristics.pdf.

Dewey, J. (1956). *The child and the curriculum*. Chicago: University of Chicago Press. (Original work published 1902).

Grapevine-Colleyville Independent School District. (2002). *Curriculum guides. Developmental characteristics*. Retrieved from www.gcisd-k12.org.

Harman, N. (2001). Student implementation of the rubric. In G. L. Taggart, S. J. Phifer, J. A. Nixon, and M. Wood (Eds.), *Rubrics: A handbook for construction and use* (pp. 37–44). Lanham, MD: Scarecrow Press.

Jalongo, M. R. (2003). *Early childhood language arts* (3rd ed.). Boston: Allyn and Bacon.

Nelson Elementary School, Columbia, SC. (2004). Third grade curriculum. Retrieved January 23, 2005: www.richland2.org/ne/currguide3.html.

PBS Parents (2011). Child development tracker. Retrieved May 5, 2011 from www.pbs.org/parents/childdevelopment/.

Tompkins, G. (2010). *Literacy for the 21st century* (5th ed.). Upper Saddle River, NJ: Merrill Prentice Hall.

Chapter 4

Using Rubrics in the Intermediate Grades

When I approach a child, he inspires in me two sentiments; tenderness for what he is, and respect for what he may become.

—Louis Pasteur

Ask teachers of grades four and five what sentiments their students inspire, and although none may answer as Pasteur did, the answers are usually as varied as the students themselves. However, many teachers do reply that they love the fact that, in some ways, these students of ages 9 and 10 are still "little kids anxious to please" but can often be given more responsibility and independence because they have the desire to be "grown-up." As one fourth-grade teacher said, "You can do such interesting things with fourth grade. I wish I could teach a whole school of fourth graders. I love them every year!"

At this age, students are moving from the early childhood literacy periods of "learning to read" to the late childhood and adult "reading to learn" stages that will be with them throughout adulthood (Chall, 1996, orig. 1983). As students enter into this age of "reading to learn," the curriculum is well suited to assessment by rubrics of all types, including rubrics that encourage self-assessment and peer assessment. This chapter presents information on the developmental characteristics of students in grades four and five, discusses the curriculum needs of these grades, and provides samples of scoring rubrics to support assessment.

DEVELOPMENTAL CHARACTERISTICS
OF FOURTH AND FIFTH GRADERS

Social Characteristics

Usually ages 9, 10, or 11, children in fourth and fifth grades are characterized by a sense of truthfulness and dependability often accompanied by a sense of innocence. This apparent innocence and bold honesty is often accompanied by the need to be part of a group. School-based clubs, such as those for stamp collecting or chess playing, are important at this level and can help to defuse the forming of inappropriate cliques that are often seen in fifth grade. In addition, clubs can help to foster and develop the wide range of interests and abilities that both fourth and fifth graders exhibit (Pennington, 2010; Wagoner, 2004; Wood, 1997).

Because their peer group is so influential at this age, fourth and fifth graders do exceptionally well using rubrics for peer assessment. (Some of the cognitive, social, and physical characteristics of children in fourth and fifth grades are listed in box 4.1.) As students gain an awareness of peer and adult expectations in these grades, they are quick to memorize rules and complain about things being "not fair." As teachers attempt to fairly assess the variety of hands-on projects so important at this age, scoring rubrics are a must to document the impartiality of the grading process.

Other social characteristics of this age that support the use of scoring rubrics include the ability to set personal goals and the willingness to assume responsibility for actions. Teachers who display rubrics on classroom walls are stimulating and encouraging both goal setting and personal responsibility.

Box 4.1 Developmental Characteristics of Intermediate Students

Cognitive Development

Age 9

- Likes to work hard
- Still needs concrete objects for understanding
- Self-critical
- Can set goals
- Discouraged by failure
- Less imaginative
- May experience "learning plateau"
- Reasons using cause and effect (If . . . then statements)

Age 10

- Likes rules and logic
- Classifies and collects
- Likes to organize
- Longer attention span
- Proud of academic products •
- Likes to achieve simple goals
- Enjoys school
- Cooperative, competitive and inquisitive

Age 11

- Likes new projects
- Able to reason abstractly
- Can set goals
- Likes to establish and modify rules
- Increased ability to see other points of view
- Likes ownership of decisions

Social Development

Age 9

- Highly competitive
- Wants to succeed
- Honest
- Focus on self
- Impatient
- Age of negatives ("boring")
- Becoming sexually aware (tells "dirty" jokes)
- Fairness important

Age 10

- Fairness crucial
- Quick to anger, quick to forgive
- Both family and peers are important
- Sense of right and wrong
- Assumes responsibility for choices
- Cooperative and competitive

- Sensitive to criticism
- Begins hero worship

Age 11

- Moody; sensitive
- Oppositional; loves to argue
- Impulsive
- Rude
- Difficulty with decisions
- Appreciates humor
- Imitates adult language
- Likes consistency
- Peer approval (including opposite sex) very important

Physical Development

Age 9

- Increased coordination until growth spurt
- Understands safety issues
- Pushes self to physical limits
- Tension outlets such as nail biting often occur

Age 10

- Large-muscle development
- Growth spurt often precedes puberty
- Growth rates vary (all sizes and shapes!)
- Handwriting often sloppier than at 9
- Snacks and rest periods helpful for growing bodies

Age 11

- Vast appetite for food; needs more sleep
- Personal hygiene issues
- Growth spurt of early adolescence, especially girls
- Restless; need to move
- Physical aggression not uncommon

Source: Adapted from Grapevine-Colleyville Independent School District, 2002; Pennington, 2010; Wagoner, 2004; Wood, 1997.

Cognitive Characteristics

Goal setting is often mentioned as a remedy for another interesting characteristic of this grade, the "fourth-grade learning plateau" or the "fourth-grade slump" (Chall, 1996, orig. 1983). According to human development theorist, Jean Piaget (1972, orig. 1924), early adolescents often become so preoccupied with the self that they exclude all else, including the acquiring of new knowledge, which then results in a mental plateau.

Others reason that the block to learning at this age is due to the increased difficulty of the subject matter as students move from learning to read to reading to learn. The vocabulary used in fourth and fifth grade textbooks becomes more difficult and less familiar (Tompkins, 2009). As students become frustrated by their lack of success, many simply turn off their learning. However, creating rubrics that list attainable goals for the all students may just provide the academic "slump breaker" that is needed for the frustrated student.

READING FLUENCY ASSESSMENT

Fluency in reading is vital at this age, and the failure to identify students who lack this fluency before the critical fourth grade level has also been cited as contributing to the learning plateau (Tompkins, 2009). One way to increase reading fluency is for teachers to post a simple checklist in the classroom that asks students four questions:

- Does my reading sound as if I'm just talking?
- Does my reading sound interesting?
- Do I pay attention to punctuation?
  or Do I
    pause at commas (,)?
    stop at periods (.)?
    make my voice ask a question at a question mark (?)?
    make my voice excited at an exclamation point (!)?
- Do I correct mistakes quickly? (Pikulski and Chard, 2005; Tompkins, 2010).

Listening to simple tape recordings of their own oral reading can help students to self-assess fluency by using the above four items on an individual checklist. Teachers wanting to assess for fluency in oral reading may use that same simple four-question guideline.

Although many experts recognize and acknowledge a plateau of learning in these grades, accountability pressure is still on for high standardized test scores and federally mandated testing. And even though these teachers are under as much pressure for student achievement as the teachers in primary grades, local resources are often diverted to all-day kindergartens and other primary programs. For example, Pennsylvania recently reported that more than half of the state's federal grant money was used for full-day kindergarten (Reeger, 2005).

While the current emphasis is on the primary student, the curriculum for the intermediate grades continues to grow. Sample curriculum summaries are listed below. This list represents only 2 of the 13 curricular areas and 27 of the total 74 benchmarks expected for fourth graders. We can see that fourth grade students are expected to

- Demonstrate interest in reading for enjoyment and to gather information.
- Choose literature and informational material appropriate to own reading skill.
- Read appropriate material with understanding from a variety of genres.
- Use reference materials to extend knowledge.
- Recall main ideas and important details from reading materials.
- Choose from a repertoire of decoding and comprehension strategies to unlock meaning of unknown words.
- Engage in all steps of the writing process; use a variety of organizational strategies to compose (e.g., word webs, outlines).
- Write for a variety of purposes and audiences; compose in narrative, descriptive, and expository styles.
- Persevere through the writing process; edit own work for punctuation, spelling, basic grammar, and paragraphing.
- Incorporate feedback from others into written compositions; provide others with feedback.
- Spell grade-level words accurately.
- Use legible cursive handwriting.
- Use a computer as a writing tool.

Under number sense and operations, this same fourth grader must

- Know addition and subtraction facts to 20.
- Round whole numbers through the millions.
- Add and subtract 4-digit numbers with and without regrouping.
- Know multiplication facts to 12 times 12.
- Know division facts up to 144 divided by 12.

- Multiply a multi-digit number by a two-digit number.
- Divide a multi-digit number by a one-digit number.
- Factor whole numbers up to 100.
- Recognize and generate equivalent forms of commonly used fractions and decimals.
- Identify on a number line the relative position of fractions, mixed numbers, and decimals to two decimal places.
- Explain different interpretations of fractions (i.e., parts of a whole or set, division, equivalents).
- Add and subtract decimals to two places. (Palo Alto Unified School District, 2004)

RUBRICS IN GRADES FOUR AND FIVE

Cognitively, students in grades four and five take pride in their finished products and enjoy rules and details. These characteristics provide a positive environment for the structure that assessments with scoring rubrics provide. Since scoring rubrics provide that blueprint for success, having this detailed list and samples of acceptable and unacceptable performance can actually help students to climb out of that learning slump. As one fourth-grader told his teacher, "It's like having a map to get you to the end of the work."

A fifth grade teacher who claimed, "I don't use rubrics for my assignments," is denying her students access to the information she possesses on how they are expected to perform. They are on a trip to unknown territory with no map, no compass, no GPS. In the same breath, she went on, "Of course, I have all these rubrics from the state standards. Who could ever use these?"

At this point she produced a folder of reading, writing, and math rubrics all provided by her school district and state department of education. These were familiar types of 4-point rubrics with assessment criteria for teachers to use. The vocabulary used was beyond any of her fifth graders. For example, the 3-point benchmark score in an analytic writing rubric stated under organization that writing at this level had a "functional arrangement of content that sustains a logical order with some evidence of transitions" (Pennsylvania Department of Education, 2003–2004).

This teacher knows that this use of terminology may squash her students' desire to write, so rather than scare them off or take the time to rewrite the rubric in simple language, she chooses not to use rubrics at all. Although her point of view is understandable, across town, her colleagues' classrooms reflect a different attitude. Posted on the back wall in the fourth and fifth grade rooms are general holistic rubrics for math and homework and a writing checklist.

Box 4.2 Homework Rubric

Homework Rubric

4. WOW! Exceptional Work (Knocks my socks off!)
     Did more than expected
3. Did what was expected (All work completed.)
     Neat and easy to read
     Name, date, page numbers
     On time
2. Did LESS than what was expected
     Difficult to read
     No name
     May be on time or may be late
1. Incomplete
     No name or date
     Almost impossible to read
     Late
0. Did nothing

Source: Reprinted with permission: L. Hoffman, Norwin School District, North Huntingdon, Pennsylvania (personal communication, May 13, 2011).

Box 4.2 contains a generic rubric to use for all homework assignments. This veteran teacher revealed that she never liked to assign letter grades to homework. However, she still wanted students to do homework, do their best, and be accountable. She likes using the rubric in box 4.3.

The homework rubric states that the 4 is so good that it knocks the teacher's socks off—it represents more than was assigned. The 3 points lists the criteria that all work is completed, a full heading (name, date, subject, page numbers) is on the paper, it is neat and legible, and on time. (If a teacher is locked into thinking of letter grades, the 3 would often be interpreted as an A and the 4 as an A plus.)

The scores of 2 points or 1 point simply state how the student failed to meet the expectation. The zero is reserved for the student who did not attempt the assignment. Although this teacher wants correct answers, that really is not the focus of this homework rubric. She is more concerned that her students get into the habit of completing the assignments neatly and on time, and the rubric reflects these goals.

The holistic math rubric below is clear and concise and yet is generic enough to be consistent with most state standards.

GENERIC MATH RUBRIC

4. Did more than required
3. All parts answered accurately and completely as required
2. Minor errors
1. Major errors
0. Did not attempt

When students are required to explain how they got their answers, this rubric provides for the correct explanation in the benchmark score of three points. When students do more or perhaps develop a creative way to solve the problem, they earn a four. The 2 and 1 for minor and major errors are vague enough to allow for teacher discretion yet can be added to for each unique assignment. For example, at the beginning of learning long division, an error in computation may be considered minor, but in a review section on division, that same error may now be considered major.

WRITING CHECKLIST

A writing checklist for this grade level asks students to check their writing for:

- many varieties in sentence structure,
- correct grammar and usage (capitalization and punctuation),
- correct spelling,
- the use of important vocabulary that adds zip to their work.

The teacher revealed that by the second half of the year, he has transitioned this list into a rubric for self-scoring. A simple format to adapt for self-assessment is illustrated in box 4.3 and lists the points as being more than

---

Box 4.3 Self-Assessment Rubric   •

Evaluation of my _____

(Assignment)

4 = I did more than was expected—better than my best work.
3 = I did what was expected—my best work.
2 = I did less than what was expected—not always my best work.
1 = I did only a small part of the assignment.
0 = I did not do this assignment at all.

Look for: (*Teacher and class determine and list critical elements for the assignment and list them in this section with an area for recording scores.*)

   Student Signature _____   Date _____

Source: Adapted with permission of the author: Laase, 1997, p. 99.

expected, what was expected, less than expected, only part of the assignment, or none at all.

Since students at this age are capable of self-assessing, the generic self-assessment rubric in box 4.3 can be adapted for many subjects and uses. When introducing self-assessment, the top section of this rubric can be used alone. Again, the teacher should model the self-assessment procedure and demonstrate what work would be "more than" and "less than" expected. Some teachers continue to use just the top area of this rubric as a holistic assessment to help students gain comfort in self-assessing. Other teachers find it helpful to analyze the assignment and list specific descriptors on the bottom section of the rubric.

Because students in these grades, especially fifth graders, are beginning to rebel against top-down directives, it is often wise to request student input as to what they value in the assignment. Empowering students to add to the assessment criteria can provide the teacher with revealing information about her scholars.

One fifth-grade teacher, who always included neatness as part of her rubric, was coaxed by her charming students to eliminate neatness as a requirement on one writing project. "Just this one time, let us be sloppy," they begged. Although she was reluctant, she agreed and was totally surprised by how neat the projects were. For some of her students, in particular those with attention disorders, these papers were their neatest ever. They were delighted by her surprise and she graciously agreed to score many with 4s for "more than expected."

Other teachers have found this self-assessment rubric to be a useful document to attach to work samples placed in student portfolios. In addition to helping students and teachers decide what documents to place in portfolios, the student's self-assessment can be a critical component for parent-teacher or student-led conferences. Simply asking students to support their decisions with explanations can open the door for parent-student communication.

The ability of 9- and 10-year-olds to comprehend more mature humor can also provide a basis for some fun rubrics with students in the intermediate grades as illustrated in box 4.4.

Box 4.4 Mascot-Writing Rubric

6 points

- The TOP! You've got all the right moves! It doesn't get any better than this! You are the true (Mascot name here).
- Extraordinary details, many examples, organized, dazzles readers and knocks both their socks off!
- Good beginning, fat middle, interesting ending, much creativity.

5 points

- Super, Duper (Mascot name here). You're on your way to the top. Next time, put the pedal to the metal (or jump on your horse) and bring it on home.
- Super details, several examples, organized, has pizzazz (knocks one sock off!).
- Beginning, fat middle, interesting ending, creativity.

4 points

- Whew-eee! We hear you (barking, growling, shouting, etc.) loud and clear. Next time impress us with a little more pizzazz. Strut your stuff. Go, (Mascot name)!
- Good details, uses examples, is organized, needs more pizzazz.
- Beginning, fat middle, ending, some creativity.

3 points

- Looking better! We know what you're trying to say. Next time put some more meat on the bones.
- Adequate but lacks completeness and sparkle, some details.
- Beginning, middle, ending.

2 points

- You're trying! Now let's get organized. Next time let's see a few more juicy details and examples. You can do it!
- Inadequate, illogical, frequent errors, some details.
- Beginning, skinny middle, maybe an ending.

1 point

- You're still in the doghouse, (Mascot name)! You tried a little bit, but you need more snap, crackle, and pop!
- Very little written, no organization, few details, errors.
- Short beginning and tiny middle.

0 points

- I'm "outta" here! There's nothing here to score, dude, or you got totally off topic. You can do better, for sure.
- Nothing written on topic, not able to score.
- NO beginning, middle, or end.

Source: Adapted with permission from: Forney, 2001.

This mascot-writing rubric can be adapted by adding whatever mascot is appropriate for your area. Teachers in a Florida school used this writing rubric with an alligator mascot, while schools in other states may use bulldogs, lions, or hawks to fill in the mascot area. Since fourth and fifth graders love being part of a group, using a school or a classroom mascot on their scoring rubrics helps to fulfill to that social need.

In some districts, the elementary school stops at grade four, and fifth graders move on to an intermediate school building or even the middle school. Whether these students are the top dogs or the lowly rookies often has an influence on behavior. Fifth graders who are part of a middle school must deal with changing classes and a variety of teachers. This is often a major change for these students who have been relocated from a small elementary school to a much larger middle school. This change of environment for a 10-year-old can result in fear, frustration, and confusion.

Producing a behavior rubric early on sets expectations no matter where these students rank in the school hierarchy. To help these students, one middle school team of fifth grade teachers developed an easy-to-understand good citizenship rubric that is illustrated below. These posters are hanging in each fifth grade classroom, and teachers are consistent in reminding students when they do and do not follow these simple procedures.

GOOD CITIZENSHIP RUBRIC

4 = always, 3 = almost always, 2 = sometimes, 1 = seldom, 0 = never

Preparation

Arrives to class on time _____

Has all materials _____

Homework complete _____

Respect

Listens when others are speaking _____

Respects other's property _____

Responds appropriately (no abusive language) _____

Follows directions _____

(Source: Adapted with permission: Hillcrest Intermediate School, Norwin School District, North Huntingdon, Pennsylvania, personal communication, May 18, 2011.)

As one teacher said, "It's good for them to be caught being good, so we make an effort to compliment students who are working on these basic guidelines." In addition, these guidelines are flexible. Teachers meet periodically to decide if the rules are working or if more specific descriptors need to be included. For example, because the teachers saw an increase in the use of abusive language among their students, the item of responding appropriately was added to the list.

Parents of fourth and fifth graders are also adjusting to the changes in their "babies" and the increase in academic difficulty. One area where this can be most obvious is in writing. Administrators preparing for state assessments in writing would be wise to inform fourth and fifth grade parents of minimal requirements.

As one fourth-grade mom whose school district had done poorly on writing assessments revealed, "I wish we [parents] had a rubric. If they [teachers and administrators] would send one home, we could actually figure out how to help our kids." Some schools have taken up that challenge and now provide websites with writing rubrics for student and parent use. Rubrics such as these help parents, students, and teachers to work as one team with clear expectations for achievement.

SUMMARY

Using rubrics in the intermediate grades can provide a vehicle for academic achievement and social growth. Having guidelines for teacher expectations empowers students to self-assess, review, and revise their work. In addition, rubrics provide a basis for personal goal setting and can provide an impetus for students to move beyond the characteristic mental plateau or learning slump of the intermediate grades. Encouraging student input in rubric design can be a powerful beginning to academic and social reflection for this age. When teachers and administrators share scoring rubric information with parents, they help to foster a team spirit for encouraging student accomplishment.

This chapter provided information on the developmental characteristics of children in grades four and five and typical curricular benchmarks for these grades. Examples of scoring rubrics appropriate for use in the intermediate grades were provided.

REFERENCES

Chall, J. S. (1983, 1996). *Stages of reading development.* New York: Harcourt Brace.

Forney, M. (2001). *Razzle-dazzle writing: Achieving excellence through 50 target skills.* Gainesville, FL: Maupin House.

Grapevine-Colleyville Independent School District (2002). *Curriculum guides. Developmental characteristics.* Retrieved February 23, 2005: www.gcisd-k12.org.

Laase, L. (1997). Let kids in on how you grade. *Instructor 106*(5), 98–99.

Palo Alto Unified School District (2004). *Fourth Grade Curriculum 2004–2005.* Retrieved February 9, 2005: www.pausd.palo-alto.ca.us/parents/curriculum/index .shtml.

Pennington, M. (2010). Free resources on developmental characteristics of learners. Retrieved May 2, 2011: penningtonpublishing.com/blog/reading/free-resources-on-developmental-characteristics-of-learners/.

Pennsylvania Department of Education (2003–2004). *The Pennsylvania System of School Assessment: Writing Assessment Handbook.* Harrisburg: Pennsylvania Department of Education.

Piaget, J. (1924, 1972). *Judgment and reasoning in the child.* Savage, MD: Littlefield, Adams and Co.

Pikulski, J.J. and Chard, D.J. (2005). Fluency: Bridge between decoding and reading comprehension. *The Reading Teacher, 58,* 510–19.

Reeger, J. (2005, February 2). Officials laud kindergarten programs. *Greensburg Tribune Review*, B1, B2.

Tompkins, G. (2010). *Literacy for the 21st century: A balanced approach.* (5th ed.). Upper Saddle River, NJ: Merrill Prentice Hall.

Wagoner, S. (2004). Developmental characteristics of youth: Implications for experiential learning. Retrieved May 2, 2011 from www.experientiallearning.ucdavis.edu/tlbx-ages.shtml.

Wood, C. (1997). *Yardsticks: Children in the classroom ages 4–14: A resource for parents and teachers.* Greenfield, MA: Northeast Foundation for Children.

Chapter 5

Using Rubrics in Middle School or Junior High School

> The mascot for every middle school should be a chameleon on a roller coaster.
>
> —A former middle school teacher

When a middle school teacher was asked about her coffee mug that screamed, "Red Alert, Red Alert; Mood Swing, Mood Swing," she replied, "It's more for the kids than for me." She explained that she's never quite sure which personality of her students she will see on a given day or how many changes of student mood may appear in a single class period. Ironically, these quick-change artists are both the "pro and con" of teaching in the middle.

Unlike their elementary counterparts, these "young adults" do not mirror the teacher's attitude, and often teachers are faced with the dilemma of how to motivate and inspire these students in grades six through eight. "During grades six to eight, young people are more likely stay in school if they like it there. And they are more likely to like it there if they feel safe, if they feel someone cares for them there, if they have successes there, and if their friends . . . and family are proud of what they achieve there" (Scales, 1996a, p. 226).

Research has shown that young people who are having difficulties in school are likely to also be having problems in other aspects of life (Ketterlinus, Lamb, Nitz, and Elster, 1992). This puts an awesome responsibility on our middle school educators to build a responsive program for each of their students (Scales, 1996b; Wiles, Bondi, and Wiles, 2006). One important component of any program that responds to the needs of students—the need for security, caring, and success—is the appropriate assessment of student achievement.

In addition to descriptions of scoring rubrics used for appropriate assessment for the students in the middle, this chapter presents information on the developmental characteristics of early adolescents, describes the characteristics of successful middle level teachers, discusses the social and curriculum needs of these grades, and provides examples of middle level scoring rubrics that teachers have used to support assessment.

DEVELOPMENTAL CHARACTERISTICS
OF EARLY ADOLESCENTS

Whether the sign outside the building says "Middle School" with its usual configuration of grades 6–8 (some include grades 5 and/or 9 also) or "Junior High School" with its usual arrangement of grades 7–9, the students in these buildings usually range in age from 11 to 14 and share the common characteristics of early adolescence. As students enter into this age of identity crisis, their attitudes and goals are changing as rapidly as their moods.

When human development theorist Erik Erikson (1963) described the conflict associated with the adolescent stage of life, he described it as "identity versus role confusion" and stated that the identity conflict present in this period is the most significant conflict that persons face throughout their lifetimes. It is sometimes obvious that these students are trying to decide just *who* they are and *what* their role in life is to be. The conflict occurs when students have different visions of these two concepts.

Teachers who have spent their entire careers teaching in the middle grades witness this conflict daily. A veteran seventh grade teacher walked into her classroom and observed one of her best students leaping from desktop to desktop. Appalled, she immediately sentenced him to a week of lunch with her in her classroom. During one of the lunches, she became curious and asked him why he had been jumping from desk to desk. He looked her in the eye and said, "Honestly, Mrs. Mains, I have no idea." And he probably was telling the truth; he could not give a reason for his actions. It was just something he did as part of his "who and what" conflict.

Teachers are not alone in witnessing this conflict. Parents often have interesting stories about students at this age. One illustration of the conflict of two "personalities" is told by a teacher friend. It seems that her 13-year-old son expressed rebellion about her requirement to attend church with her. His reaction was to dress for church every week in old jeans and a T-shirt. Although she did not like it, she chose not to argue about it. When, during the service, the minister revealed that the ushers needed a volunteer to take up the collection, her blue-jean-clad son immediately jumped up to help. "Honestly," she revealed, "I wasn't sure if I should be proud or ashamed!"

Because students of this age need their own "space," their bedroom often becomes another source of conflict. Although the early adolescent becomes painfully aware of neatness in appearance, the same is often not apparent in the bedroom, where the challenge may be to see any part of the carpeting. One parent observed, "Even the dog won't go in there." The overflow of this sloppiness often extends to schoolwork, where the objective may be to finish—with or without quality.

Box 5.1 illustrates some of the developmental characteristics of middle level learners from ages 12 to 14. (Age 11 is included in box 4.1, Developmental Characteristics of Intermediate Students, in chapter 4.)

Box 5.1 Developmental Characteristics of Middle School Students (See box 4.1 in chapter 4 for 11-year-olds.)

Cognitive Development

Age 12

- Increased ability to think in abstract terms.
- Can and will see both sides to an argument.
- High interest in current events, politics, social justice; also pop culture, materialism.

Age 13

- Abstract reasoning and "formal operations" *begin to be* functional in some at age 13
- Not willing to take big learning risks (adolescent insecurity).
- Likes to challenge intellectual as well as social authority .
- Physical demands of puberty may slow intellectual growth.

Age 14

- More abstract reasoning evident, especially in regard to cause and effect.
- More willing to admit an error and revise their work.
- Learns well in cooperative groups.
- Responds well to academic variety and challenge.
- Easily bored.
- Interested in the meaning of words; developing a broader vocabulary.

Social Development

Age 12

- Adult personality begins to emerge.
- Enthusiastic, uninhibited.
- Self-aware, insightful.
- Can set realistic goals in the short term.
- Peers more important than teachers.
- Concerned with rules, standards, and fairness for themselves.

Age 13

- Neatness with personal appearance, not with environment.
- Often quieter than 12s
- Like to be alone at home.
- Close friendships obviously more important to girls.
- Boys hang in groups or more formal gangs.
- Telephone, computer, video games and other electronic diversions a major time factor.
- Street language/peer language important.
- Rude occasionally.

Age 14

- Like to do as much as possible—cram much into the day as they can.
- Often embarrassed to be seen with their parents; critical of parental dress, habits, friends, ideas.
- Can be a "pain" at home and a star at school.
- Focus on self and sense of identity.
- Think others think the same as they do.

Physical Development

Age 12

- Growth spurt; signs of puberty.
- Food important, especially midmorning in school—some concerned with dieting and body image.
- Physical education and sports valued.
- High energy.
- Need for personal hygiene.

Age 13

- Skin problems emerging; hygiene a key issue.
- Girls: 95 percent of mature height; menstruation has begun for most.
- Boys: voice change for many; growth spurt about a year behind girls.
- Concerned about being "normal."

Age 14

- High energy continues.
- Loud.
- Girls: full development nearly complete.
- Boys: growth spurt continues—upper body strength developing.
- Still concerned about being "normal."

(Bucher & Manning, 2006; Feiltser & Tomonari, 2003; Grapevine-Colleyville Independent School District, 2002; Wagoner, 2004; Wiles, Bondi, & Wiles, 2006; Wood, 1997.)

The range of diversity in this list is reflected in the classroom. One eighth-grade math teacher described his students as having one foot on the bank of childhood and the other foot in the moving rowboat of adulthood. "I see them jumping back and forth between the 'bank' and the 'boat' all day long. If you can't laugh, you'll go crazy. Sometimes I just look the other way." The sewing teacher agreed: "except when the boys are treating the sewing machines like a NASCAR race. You want to laugh, but you just have to be everywhere!"

CHARACTERISTICS OF SUCCESSFUL MIDDLE LEVEL TEACHERS

The attitude of these two teachers represents the philosophies of successful teachers of early adolescents. The ideal middle level teacher combines the teaching strategies of the elementary teacher with the subject-specific academic rigor of the high school teacher. As one university dean of a teacher preparation program described them, "A middle school teacher must have the subject knowledge of the high school teacher with the heart of the elementary teacher."

These teachers of grades five through nine must be child centered, must be team players, and must use a variety of hands-on methods. Although

competence in subject matter is important, many educators believe that teachers can always learn academic content matter. However, the child-centered,
caring attitude so needed by middle school teachers is difficult to teach
(George, Stevenson, Thomason, and Beane, 1992).

In addition to this caring attitude, the exemplary middle school teacher must
possess a thorough knowledge of the developmental characteristics of young
people from ages 10 to 14. This knowledge of young adolescence must be
accompanied by an attitude of acceptance of these young people (George et al.,
1992; Midgley and Anderman, 1995; National Education Association, 1999). In
other words, to quote one adolescent, too many "school people not only don't
understand the problems we have, they can't *stand* us" (Casella, 2001, p. 14).

Other middle level students have described their ideal middle school
teacher this way: "They should be nice. They should make learning fun
and interesting. They should care about us" (Knowles and Brown, 2000,
pp. 165–66). According to the National Board for Professional Teaching
Standards (1996), a vital characteristic for middle level educators is the
knowledge of how to address the diverse needs of their students (National
Board, 1996; Reed and Rossi, 2000).

MIDDLE LEVEL CURRICULUM

To meet these diverse needs, curricular goals for the middle level can be vast,
indeed. Whether the building is labeled middle school or junior high, the
intensity of curricular requirements within its walls remains the same. This is
the level where national pressure exists for our students to compare globally
with other nations in the math and science assessments such as the Trends
in International Mathematics and Science Study (TIMSS, formerly known as
the Third International Mathematics and Science Study). A glimpse at only
part of a sample eighth-grade math standards from any state illustrates the
pressures on both students and teachers in the middle grades.

The pressure continues for standardized testing in reading, also. If the
fourth grade reading slump (see chapter 4) was never addressed in earlier
grades, it can become an enormous chasm in the middle grades.

A graduate student, reflecting on his reading past, wrote, "When we discussed the fourth grade slump, it made me realize why I hated reading from
sixth grade on. I hit that slump, but not until sixth grade. I completely remember not wanting to read anything; reading became a continuous struggle. I
constantly had to go back and reread. I got sick of reading to the point that I
didn't want to do it at all. That feeling has stayed with me, and now, in graduate school, I need to force myself to do the required readings."

USING RUBRICS IN THE MIDDLE GRADES

If rubrics have been used prior to the sixth grade, these students will be expecting the same scoring guidelines and fairness when they reach grades six to eight. However, in addition to the answer of fairness, scoring rubrics provide support for other important academic and emotional issues in the lives of early adolescents and their teachers.

Because they are moving to adulthood, many students at this age respond positively when their input is sought. Not only does it make sense to ask for students' opinions in academic areas, it provides a basis for cooperation and learning and helps to eliminate any power-struggle attitudes.

A group of middle school teachers recently listed three universal nuisances connected to assessment of middle school curriculum. These three "thorns" were getting their students to complete homework on time, having students maintain subject notebooks, and helping students with the recent emphasis on writing in all subject areas. The rubrics illustrated in boxes 5.2 through 5.6 helped to facilitate these three problem assessment areas of homework, notebooks, and writing.

RUBRICS FOR HOMEWORK, NOTEBOOKS, WRITING, AND MATH

A government publication on homework, (Paulu, n.d), tells teachers that consistent and constructive feedback on assignments is crucial if they are to portray homework as an important tool for helping students to learn. With the many demands on teachers' time, it is sometimes difficult to provide consistent feedback. However, using a homework rubric can facilitate that chore and provide students with the feedback that they need.

The analytic homework rubric illustrated in box 5.2 can be adapted for any descriptors that specific subjects may warrant. (Another sample homework rubric can be found in chapter 4, box 4.2.)

Box 5.2 Analytic Rubric for Homework

Completion of required assignment

4. All items completed beyond expectations. (Or more than required items completed.)
3. All items completed.
2. Most (at least half) of the items completed.
1. Fewer than half of the items completed.

0. No homework is submitted. Unable to evaluate.

Basic requirements (spelling, punctuation, legibility)

4. No spelling errors. No usage errors. No mechanics errors. Legible. Exceeds requirements.
3. Meets all requirements. One or two spelling, usage, or mechanics errors.
2. Meets most requirements. Three or four errors in spelling or mechanics; or difficult to read.
1. Meets few requirements. Five or more errors in spelling and usage or mechanics; illegible.
0. No homework is submitted. Unable to evaluate.

Understanding

4. Shows complete and extensive understanding of the _____.
3. Shows considerable understanding of the _____.
2. Shows developing understanding of the _____.
1. Shows little understanding of the _____.
0. No homework is submitted. Unable to evaluate.

Total score _____

Source: Adapted with permission: L. Hoffmann, teacher, Norwin Middle School, N. Huntingdon, Pennsylvania.

Under completion rate, some teachers actually list a percentage for completion such as 90, 50, or fewer than 50 percent of the items are complete. In other schools, teachers prefer to use just the completeness descriptors for one holistic rubric. In the sample in box 5.2, the basic requirements of spelling, punctuation, and legibility have been grouped together as one score; however, some teachers may choose to provide a separate score for each of those components. The category of understanding can be filled in to accommodate whatever assignment is being assessed from using the scientific method to writing a haiku.

A simple way of adapting this homework rubric to specific needs can be accomplished with student input. Students who are struggling for adult identification thrive on being given a choice and voice in assignments and assessment. Using student input makes the task a bit easier for the teacher and provides ownership of the assessment for the student. (See chapter 11 for a discussion on student-generated rubrics.)

The second nuisance assignment that this group of middle school teachers identified was the required notebook. Notebooks are linked to homework, and, as one teacher complained, "I know I should check them, but honestly, it is so time-consuming and boring. Yet I feel guilty since I know that they need to get accustomed to keeping a notebook for high school."

The notebook evaluation rubric devised and revised by a group of middle school teachers is shown in box 5.3. Students can earn a maximum of 4 points for the notebook. Teachers can modify this rubric to their own styles and areas of emphasis or to include student input.

Box 5.3 Holistic Rubric for Notebooks

Notebook Rubric

4 points

- More sections completed than required, or creativity evident.
- No spelling errors. No usage errors.
- Organization is beyond expectations.
- Notebook is kept very neat; perfect, easy to read.

3 points

- All required sections are complete.
- One or two spelling or mechanics errors.
- All assignments and/or notes are kept in a logical or numerical sequence as required.
- Overall notebook is kept in neat condition; easy to read.

2 points

- One or two required sections are missing or incomplete.
- Three or four errors in spelling, usage, or mechanics.
- One or two assignments and/or notes are not in a logical or numerical sequence.
- Overall notebook is kept in satisfactory condition.

1 point

- Three or more required sections are missing or incomplete.
- Five or more errors in spelling and usage or mechanics.

- Three or more assignments and/or notes are not in a logical or numerical sequence.
- Overall notebook is unkempt and disorganized.

0 points

- No notebook is presented.
- Unable to evaluate.

Source: Adapted with permission: L. Hoffmann, teacher, Norwin Middle School, N. Huntingdon, Pennsylvania.

Box 5.4, below, illustrates how the holistic rubric in box 5.3 can be expanded to an in-depth analytic rubric format where the student would earn a maximum of 16 points.

Box 5.4 Analytic Rubric for Notebooks

- Completion of required sections
  4. More sections completed than required, or creativity evident.
  3. All required sections are complete.
  2. One or two required sections are missing or incomplete.
  1. More than three required sections are missing or incomplete.
  0. No notebook is presented. Unable to evaluate.

- Mechanics/usage and spelling
  4. No spelling errors. No usage errors. No mechanics errors.
  3. One or two spelling, usage, or mechanics errors.
  2. Three or four errors in spelling or mechanics.
  1. Five or more errors in spelling and usage or mechanics.
  0. No notebook is presented. Unable to evaluate.

- Organization
  4. Organization is beyond expectations.
  3. All assignments and/or notes are kept in a logical or numerical sequence as required.
  2. One or two assignments and/or notes are not in a logical or numerical sequence.

1. Three or more assignments and/or notes are not in a logical or numerical sequence.
0. No notebook is presented. Unable to evaluate.

• Neatness
 4. Neat beyond expectations. Perfect.
 3. Overall notebook is kept in neat condition.
 2. Overall notebook is kept in satisfactory condition.
 1. Overall notebook is unkempt and disorganized.
 0. No notebook is presented. Unable to evaluate.

Total score _____

Source: Adapted with permission: L. Hoffmann, teacher, Norwin Middle School, N. Huntingdon, PA.

A middle school social studies teacher, who uses the analytic notebook rubric in box 5.4, believes in announcing the dates when notebooks will be collected and evaluated. She varies the dates so she's not collecting notebooks from more than two sections per day. She prefers to check them during prep periods or after school. "I have the students put their names on the rubric and slip it inside the notebook. Then all I need is a pen and a cup of tea." She added that she checks them once or twice during a nine-week grading period.

One veteran science teacher reported that his method of checking notebooks included a surprise check since students were expected to bring their notebooks to every class. He provides an in-class work assignment and collects the notebooks of those present in alphabetical order.

Using the holistic rubric in figure box 5.3, he can quickly assess all 25 notebooks and jot down points on a grade sheet in one 40-minute class period. Any notebooks that are not evaluated are saved and checked after school when points for all notebooks are entered into the grade book. (He collects the notebooks of absent students upon their return.)

The third identified grading nightmare for teachers in the middle is grading writing of all types. With the inclusion of a writing sample on the SATs (see chapter 6 for a discussion of the SAT writing rubric), middle school teachers are feeling the pressure to prepare their students for successful writing across the curriculum. Writing activities that were once limited to English class are now being produced in all subject areas including math and science. The narrative essay rubric described below asks questions that can be scored from four to zero. It is an excellent tool for assessing writing in grades six, seven, and eight in any subject.

NARRATIVE ESSAY RUBRIC QUESTIONS TO ASK

- *Focus*: Does the essay concentrate on one topic and stick to the subject?
- *Content*: Are ideas fully developed through the use of facts, examples, anecdotes, details, opinions, reasons, explanations, or dialogue? (For the narrative, I will be looking specifically for answers to the 5W's and sensory details.)
- *Organization*: Is there an interesting title? Does the introduction capture the reader's attention? Is one main idea expressed in each paragraph? Paragraphs must contain a topic sentence, supportive detaisls, and a concluding sentence. Is there a well-written conclusion?
- *Style*: Does the writer vary sentence patterns and use interesting words? ("Alot" is not a word—get rid of it!!!)
- *Conventions*: Are spelling, punctuation, capitalization, and sentence structure correct? No run-ons or sentence fragments. (Source: Reprinted with permission: Sixth grade teachers, Hillcrest Intermediate School, North Huntingdon, Pennsylvania, personal communication, May 18, 2011).

Middle school teachers who use the writing checklist below find that their students now understand what is meant by content, focus, organization, style, and conventions.

STUDENT WRITING ASSIGNMENT CHECKLIST

Student Writing Assignment Checklist

AREA	QUESTION	YES/NO
Content:	Are details specific and supportive of the topic?	_____
	Are ideas fully developed?	_____
	Does the information support the topic and focus on the theme?	_____
Focus:	Was there a specific audience?	_____
	Were all the ideas clear?	_____
	Does the writing sustain a single point of view?	_____
Organization:	Is there a definite sequence?	_____
	Does each paragraph deal with one idea?	_____
	Are sentences in logical order?	_____
	Do transitions exist between paragraphs or ideas?	_____

	Are the introductions and conclusions clear?	_____
Style:	Is the word choice effective and appropriate?	_____
	Does the structure vary?	_____
Conventions:	Are spelling, punctuation, and capitalization correct?	_____
	Is the usage correct?	_____
	Are all the sentences complete?	_____
	Are there any run-on sentences?	_____

Source: Adapted with permission: Middle level teachers, Hillcrest Intermediate School, Norwin School District, North Huntingdon, Pennsylvania (personal communication, May 18, 2011).

These two scoring tools complement each other in the analysis of good writing and have been used as both self-assessment and teacher-assessment documents.

Although assessing homework, notebooks, and writing were the top three areas suggested by one group of middle school teachers, no discussion of rubrics at any level would be complete without mentioning math. The standards written by the National Council of Teachers of Math (NCTM) support having students develop "systematic reasoning" as an integral method of teaching math at all ages (National Council of Teachers of Mathematics, 2000).

Justifying mathematical answers in writing has become required by many state assessments. Descriptors in rubrics to assess the written and oral explanations of solutions in math class range from "exemplary with clear, complete, and coherent explanations" to "partial and incomplete," all the way to "did not attempt or completely off task."

Since some standardized tests require students to write the justification of their answers in a limited area or box with points deducted for writing outside the specified area, teachers may want to add that criterion to their rubric to help students become comfortable with that limitation.

Box 5.5 contains the simple grading rubric that an experienced eighth grade math teacher created for assessing basic skills.

It covers both mathematical computation and mathematical reasoning. The teacher explained, "It has to be simple for them and for me." When asked about the fact that she had no 2s or 4s listed on the rubric, she replied, "I reserve the right to award 4s and 2s for student work in that gray area. I learned early on that there might be some [papers] that are just not that easy to classify. Math is no longer black and white—right or wrong. The rubrics help, and giving myself some leeway makes my job easier."

Box 5.5 Math Rubric for Basic Skills Assessment

Solution

5: Correct numerical solution.
3: Incorrect but reasonable numerical solution.
1: No solution or unreasonable incorrect solution.
0: Did not attempt.

Explanation

5: Full logical explanation.
3: Partial but reasonable explanation.
1: No explanation or minimal explanation.
0: Did not attempt.

Source: Reprinted with permission: T. Quinlan, middle school math teacher, Roanoke, Virginia.

SUMMARY

Using rubrics in the middle level grades can help to provide a stabilizing factor in the academic and emotional conflict of students in grades six to nine. Since students at this age value choice and voice, getting student input in assessment criteria can encourage an enthusiasm for learning and eliminate power struggles.

This chapter provided information on the developmental characteristics of young people in grades six through eight with a glimpse of curricular expectations for these students. In addition, descriptions of the characteristics of successful middle level teachers, information on the social and curriculum needs of middle grades, and examples of middle level scoring rubrics that teachers have used to support assessment were provided. Generic scoring rubrics appropriate for use in the middle grades in the assessment of homework, notebooks, writing, and math were presented.

REFERENCES

Bucher, K., and Manning, M. L. (2006). *Young adult literature: Exploration, evaluation, and appreciation.* Upper Saddle River, NJ: Pearson.

Casella, R. (2001). *At zero tolerance: Punishment, prevention, and school violence.* New York: Peter Lang.

Erikson, E. H. (1963). *Childhood and society* (2nd ed.). New York: W. W. Norton and Company.

Feiler, R. and Tomonari, D. (2003). Child development: Stages of growth. *Encyclopedia of Education.* Retrieved May 7, 2011 from www.encyclopedia.com/doc/1G2–3403200106.html.

George, P. S., Stevenson, C., Thomason, J., and Beane, J. (1992). *The middle school—and beyond.* Alexandria, VA: Association for Supervision and Curriculum Development (ASCD).

Grapevine-Colleyville Independent School District. (2002). *Curriculum guides. Developmental characteristics.* Retrieved February 23, 2005: www.gcisd-k12.org/lists/guides/currguides_main.html.

Ketterlinus, R. D., Lamb, M. E., Nitz, K., and Elster, A. B. (1992). Adolescent nonsexual and sex-related problem behaviors. *Journal of Adolescent Research,* 7(4), 431–56.

Knowles, T. and Brown, D. F. (2000). *What every middle school teacher should know.* Portsmouth, NH: Heinemann.

Midgley, C., and Anderman, E. (1995). Differences between elementary and middle school teachers and students: A goal theory approach, task or performance? *Journal of Early Adolescence, 15*(1), 90–113.

National Board for Professional Teaching Standards (2000). *Early adolescence/generalist standards for board certification.* Washington, D.C.: Author. Retrieved October 30, 2000: www.nbpts.org.

National Council of Teachers of Mathematics (NCTM). (2000). *Principles and standards for school mathematics.* Reston, VA: Author.

National Education Association. (1999). Middle schools: Something new or tried and true? *NEA Today,* 18(3), 33.

Paulu, N. (n.d). *Helping your students with homework: A guide for teachers.* Washington, DC: U.S. Government Printing Office.

Reed, D.F. and Rossi, J.A. (2000). My three wishes: Hopes, aspirations, and concerns of middle school students. *Clearing House,* 73(3), 141–44.

Scales, P. C. (1996a). A responsive ecology for positive young adolescent development. *Clearing House,* 69(4), 226–30.

Scales, P. C. (1996b). *Boxed in and bored: How middle schools continue to fail young adolescents—and what good middle schools do right.* Minneapolis, MN: Search Institute.

Wagoner, S. (2004). Developmental characteristics of youth: Implications for experiential learning. Retrieved April 4, 2011 from www.experientiallearning.ucdavis.edu/tlbx-ages.shtml.

Wiles, J., Bondi, J. and Wiles, M. T. (2006). *The essential middle school, 4ed.* Columbus, OH: Pearson.

Wood, C. (1997). *Yardsticks: Children in the classroom ages 4–14: A resource for parents and teachers.* Greenfield, MA: Northeast Foundation for Children.

Chapter 6

Using Rubrics in High School

Treat people as if they were what they ought to be and you help them to become what they are capable of being.

—Johann W. von Goethe

A high school math teacher, who had previously taught in a middle school for 10 years, told a group of his high school colleagues, "You have no idea of how good you have it." He was referring to the relative calm of his high school juniors and seniors when compared to his eighth graders.

Unlike the variety of configurations for middle schools, high schools in this country are usually configured with grade levels of either 9–12 or 10–12. Often referred to as being in the development stage of late adolescence, students in these grades are moving toward adulthood at a variety of rates, but many have left behind the mood swings of the middle grades and are seriously considering their adult roles. As the Goethe quote above indicates, high school teachers are crucial to helping these youths "become what they are capable of being."

A great part of the responsibility of helping high school students reach their full potential is making sure that all students graduate. The high school dropout rate continues to be a concern in the United States.

The *status dropout rate* (the percentage of 16- through 24-year-olds who are not enrolled in school and have not earned a high school diploma or equivalent) has steadily declined (Aud, Hussar, Planty, Snyder, Bianco, Fox, Frohlich, Kemp, and Drake, 2010). However, recent studies show that the national high school dropout rate is at 32 percent, which means that about one third of students who enter high school never finish (Paulson, 2010).

Although approximately 78 percent of White and Asian students complete high school, only 50 percent of their Hispanic or African American classmates will graduate with them. To complicate those data, the students who do graduate are not always prepared for college. Only 20 percent of Black high school graduates and 16 percent of Hispanic high school graduates are considered ready for college (Greene and Foster, 2003; Huebert and Corbett, 2005; Orfield, Losen, Wald, and Swanson, 2004).

High school teachers need strategies to reach and assess all students—even those who are contemplating dropping out. This chapter presents information on the developmental characteristics of students in grades 9–12, discusses educational resiliency, lists the characteristics of students and teachers in model high schools, and relates the curriculum needs of these grades to sample scoring rubrics to support assessment.

DEVELOPMENTAL CHARACTERISTICS OF HIGH SCHOOL STUDENTS

A substitute teacher for local high schools revealed that she could tell whether the students in any of her classes for the day are freshman as soon as they enter the classroom. The 14-year-olds who are in our high schools still have much of the exuberance and child-like behavior of the middle school. (See box 5.1 in the previous chapter for developmental characteristics of 14-year-olds.) Because high school freshman are often loud and boisterous, especially when compared with the upperclassmen, they are easily recognized.

The sophomores, juniors, and seniors, however, view life with more aloof sophistication. Box 6.1 illustrates the developmental characteristics of these students from ages 15 to 17.

Box 6.1 Developmental Characteristics of High School Students

Cognitive Development

Age 15

- Formal operational thinking developing for some students, making them more capable of abstract thinking, problem solving, and future-focused thinking.
- Concrete thinking is dominant (focused on here and now, self, and events directly experienced).
- Usually consider academic goals secondary to personal/social concerns.
- Sometimes preoccupied about problems with academic performance.

- Do not always distinguish between what others are thinking and what they are thinking themselves.
- Learn best when actively involved with ideas connected to their own personal experiences.

Age 16

- Formal operational thinking is developing, but concrete thinking is still evident for most students.
- Better able to understand the perspectives of others.
- Able to experience metacognition—the ability to know what one knows and does not know.
- Academic goals remain secondary to social concerns.
- Concerned about societal issues such as homelessness, crime, or the environment.
- Greater capacity for setting goals.
- Understanding of cause and effect is complicated by feelings of invulnerability ("It can't happen to me") and can result in dangerous, risk-taking behaviors—drinking, drugs, and so on.

Age 17

- Continuation of the development of formal operational thinking. (Note: Only about 35 percent reach this stage of formal operational stage of thinking by the end of high school.)
- Concrete thinking still is evident for most students.
- Better able to make independent decisions.
- Able to see the perspectives of others.
- More developed sense of humor.
- Becoming introspective.
- Although academic goals are becoming a reality, these are often still secondary to personal/social concerns.
- Usually interested in vocational goals.
- Able to experience metacognition—ability to know what one knows and what one does not know.

Social Development
Age 15

- Self-involvement, alternating between unrealistically high expectations and poor self-concept.

- Complain that parents interfere with independence.
- Feel unique; no one else has ever felt so much, suffered so much, loved so deeply, or been so misunderstood.
- Extremely concerned with appearance.
- Great desire for privacy.
- Development of ideals and selection of role models.
- Better control over impulsiveness.
- Strong desire to be involved in decision making about rules.
- Extremely sensitive to the norms of peer group, including choices in dress, hairstyle, vocabulary, and music.
- Testing rules and questioning authority are common.
- Increased interest in opposite sex.

Age 16

- Strong emphasis on the peer group with the group identity based on selectivity, superiority, and competitiveness.
- Greater freedom and mobility (jobs, driving, etc.).
- Still complain that parents interfere with independence.
- Break away from same-sex parent.
- Concerned with physical attractiveness.
- Effort to make new friends.
- Testing rules and questioning authority.
- Better control of impulsiveness, but risk-taking behavior evident.
- Mood swings.
- Striving for independence and autonomy is greatly increased with an increased desire for privacy.
- Becoming more self-directed.
- Periods of sadness as the psychological withdrawal from parents takes place.

Age 17

- Greater ability to think ideas through and express in words.
- Greater ability to delay gratification.
- Increased concern for others.
- Better able to compromise.
- Better ability to set goals and follow through.
- Peer relationships remain important, but becoming more self-directed.
- Increased self-reliance; better able to make independent decisions.

- Moody, maybe rebellious, seeking independence.
- Need parental respect for opinion and acceptance of maturity.
- Need acceptance by society—in job, and in college.
- Increased emphasis on personal dignity and self-esteem.
- Higher level of concern for the future.
- Relationships may be more serious.

Physical Development

Age 15

- Enormous physical development for males in weight, height, heart size, lung capacity, and muscular strength.
- Growing pains (make have stomach aches, headaches, and joint pains).
- Often tired and hungry.
- Bone growth is exceeding muscle growth, resulting in poor coordination and awkwardness (especially for males).
- Ravenous appetite and peculiar tastes.
- Fluctuations in basal metabolism cause restlessness and lethargy.

Age 16

- Physical growth nearing completion; reaching adult development.
- Generally have poorer health, lowered levels of endurance, strength, and flexibility.
- Usually heavier than previous ages.
- Physically more at risk from accidents, suicides, and homicides.
- Multiple hormones responsible for mood swings.
- Concerned about body; worry about being normal.

Age 17

- Multiple hormones responsible for mood swings.
- Physical growth nearing completion, reaching adult development.
- Generally have poorer health, lowered level of flexibility.
- Fluctuations in basal metabolism continuing.
- Sleep requirements approaching adult levels.

(Bucher &Manning, 2006;Feiler & Tomonari, 2003; Grapevine-Colleyville Independent School District, 2002; Wagoner, 2004.)

Socially, peer groups are still of primary importance for ages 15 and 16. By 17, however, students are looking more to society for acceptance as they contemplate entering the job market or college. Adding to this transition to adulthood is the fact that this is the age when romantic relationships may become more serious.

Cognitively, formal operational thinking is developing in high school students, which means that students are gaining in the abilities to predict possible consequences of events, to see consequences of their actions, to argue contrary to fact, and to think without egocentrism (thinking about the whole and not just the self).

However, it should be noted that only about 35 percent of high school seniors reach this stage of abstract thinking that enables clear focus on the future (Jensen, 2005). With more than 65 percent of high school students still working in the egocentric concrete thinking mode for the majority of the school day, teachers at this level are quick to recognize that their students are "still kids" no matter how grown-up they appear.

An interesting comment from a high school sophomore suggested that high school teachers "should not treat us [students] as little kids even though we still are kids." As high school teachers experiment with strategies to motivate and encourage these "adult-kids," the concrete formula of a scoring rubric can help with student quality and assessment, especially for students who are not yet comfortable with thinking in the abstract.

EDUCATIONAL RESILIENCY

Much has been written on the "educational resilience" of successful students. Educational resilience has been defined as "the heightened likelihood of educational success despite personal vulnerabilities and adversities brought about by environmental conditions and experience" (Wang, Haertel, and Walberg, 1997, p. 119). In other words, educational resilience is that quality in children who, despite many adverse situations in their lives, succeed in school.

These resilient students, who would be labeled "at risk," do not engage in the activities usually associated with school failure such as drug and alcohol abuse or delinquency. Instead, they succeed. Now, as an alternative for focusing on the characteristics that place a child at risk, educators are questioning and examining the attributes of students who succeed against all odds.

Four personal attributes common to resilient students have been identified. These four attributes are *social competence, the ability to solve problems, independence*, and *a sense of purpose*.

Teachers who promote resilience have been identified as teachers who *demonstrate caring, set high expectations, offer support* to reach those expectations, *provide opportunities for meaningful connections* of subject matter, and *practice effective student-centered instruction* (Topf, Frazier-Maiwald, and Krovetz, 2004). (See chapter 11 for details on effective student-centered instruction.)

Because educational resiliency can be developed, teachers at the high school level are encouraged to create environments of collegiality, respect, and choice and voice that help students "reach for the best version of themselves" (Sizer and Sizer, 1999, p. xiii).

RUBRICS IN HIGH SCHOOL

In Kathleen Cushman's (2003) *Fires in the Bathroom: Advice for Teachers from High School Students*, high school students are quoted giving advice to teachers. In the chapter on respect and trust, the students are often quoted as advising teachers to grade them fairly. Their comments include, "If someone gives you a bad grade, they should tell you exactly why" (p. 27), and "The worst thing for a teacher to be considered is unfair" (p. 34).

When another group of high school students was asked what constituted "teacher fairness," their responses echoed the responses of the students in Cushman's (2003) book. Their advice on fairness for high school teachers actually supports the characteristics for both educational resiliency and using rubrics to assess student work. These fair teachers' characteristics include such basics as making expectations clear, making sure all students understand, grading fairly, setting high expectations (and helping students to meet those expectations), giving feedback, and understanding that students make errors.

Because these students are willing to admit to errors and can revise work accordingly, the feedback from a scoring rubric can address issues of both fairness and respect.

COOPERATIVE GROUP RUBRICS

Fairly grading cooperative group activities is often a dilemma for teachers. The rubric illustrated in box 6.2 was submitted by high school social studies teachers who use it to assess the group effort of a variety of small group activities. The rubric is used for students to assess each group member and to assess their own contributions. It can be adapted for any group activity at any level.

As one teacher explained the group rubric, the first and last criteria of participation and cooperation are constant. "The tasks change as the assignment changes, and I can change those [tasks] to fit any activity. Students are required to complete this in private and know that, although I will address any group problems, their responses will remain confidential."

Because the teacher stresses the importance of teamwork in real-world occupations, students take this rubric seriously and respond honestly. The addition of having students reflect upon and assess their own contribution helps to ensure group cooperation.

Box 6.2 Group Evaluation Rubric

Your name _____

Group Evaluation

Directions:

Write each group member's name in the indicated line. Then, rate each group member according to how they participated in the activity. Use the following scale to rate the group members *and yourself.*

Scoring guide: 2 = often; 1 = sometimes; 0 = never

Group member _____

- Participated in discussion   Score _____
- Task one: (*Teacher specifies task here*)   Score _____
- Task two: (*Teacher specifies task here*)   Score _____
- Task three: (*Teacher specifies task here*)   Score _____
- Helped maintain a positive work environment
  (willingness to cooperate and share workload)   Score _____

                                        Total score _____

Comments:

Source: Adapted with permission: Southmoreland School District, Scottdale, PA.

ORAL PRESENTATIONS

Box 6.3 contains a rubric used for an oral or written presentation and was created by a teacher in a foods and nutrition course for high school students.

Box 6.3 Analytic Rubric for Oral Presentation

- Focus
    4. Tells one idea, sticks to the topic, makes sense.
    3. Tells one idea, sticks to the topic for most of the script, makes sense.
    2. Tells one idea, keeps on the topic fairly well and makes sense for most of the presentation.
    1. Has no main idea, does not keep to the topic well, and makes little or no sense.
    0. No work is submitted. Unable to evaluate.

- Content
    4. Ideas are fully developed through fact and detail.
    3. Ideas are developed for most of the ad through fact and details.
    2. Ideas are not fully developed in all areas of fact and detail.
    1. No clear development of fact and details in presentation.
    0. No work is submitted. Unable to evaluate.

- Organization
    4. Ideas flow in an orderly fashion with a well-written script or ad copy.
    3. Ideas flow in a somewhat orderly fashion with a well-written script or ad copy.
    2. Ideas do not flow well throughout ad copy or script.
    1. No apparent main idea, and a poorly written script or ad copy.
    0. No work is submitted. Unable to evaluate.

- Style
    4. Clearly understood and well organized presentation of ad copy. Well written script with good sentence structure.
    3. Ad copy is fairly well organized and is understandable. Script is written with only one or two corrections needed in structure of sentences.
    2. Ad copy is understandable but could use improvement in organization. Script is written with three or four corrections needed in sentence structure.
    1. Ad copy is difficult to interpret or read. Inappropriate word and sentence structure used in script.
    0. No work is submitted. Unable to evaluate.

- Conventions
    4. Correct grammar/mechanics used throughout all copy or script.
    3. Proper grammar mostly used with one or two allowances for error.
    2. Proper grammar used with three or four allowances for error.
    1. Script contains five or more errors in grammar/mechanics.
    0. No work is submitted. Unable to evaluate.

- Presentation
    4. Presentation is clear and easily understood by the audience.
    3. Presentation is clear for most of the presentation and understood by the audience.
    2. Presentation is partially clear but not completely understandable.
    1. Presentation is difficult to understand and not clear.
    0. No work is submitted. Unable to evaluate.

                                        Total score _____

Source: Reprinted with permission: S. Trenk, family and consumer sciences student teacher, Norwin High School, North Huntingdon, Pennsylvania.

Although the assignment was to create and present an advertisement for a nutritional component such as a specific vitamin or mineral, the rubric can be adapted for presentations in other academic areas.

The main areas listed in the rubric (focus, content, organization, style, and conventions) are consistent with writing rubrics and checklists used by English and language arts teachers in middle and elementary levels. (See chapter 5, box 5.6, for a writing assignment checklist for middle school.) This consistency across the curriculum and grade levels provides a strong foundation for achievement for students. When students are comfortable with and recognize the terms of the requirements, they approach assignments with more confidence and resulting increased self-efficacy.

Under the area of style on this rubric, the teacher provided an opportunity for an alternative to the oral presentation. Because she recognized the students' need for "choice and voice" in the assignment, the teacher included the option of having students create a print ad or an oral advertisement. In addition to giving the students a choice in the assignment, this "either-or" in only one category helped students to see the close relationship between written and oral presentations. Whether students chose to do the written or the oral, the guidelines were the same in four of the five areas of assessment.

Rubrics for oral presentations that are assisted by technology are created at each grade level. A sample high school PowerPoint presentation rubric is discussed in chapter 9.

RUBRICS TO ASSESS WRITING

The emphasis on writing at the high school level is illustrated by both the writing requirements of No Child Left Behind (NCLB) and the Scholastic Aptitude Test (SAT). Both have requirements for writing and assess that writing by the use of scoring rubrics. The required SAT short essay is described as measuring student ability to "organize and express ideas clearly, develop and support the main idea, and use appropriate word choice and sentence structure" (SAT Writing Section, 2011).

The SAT Scoring Guide lists the 6-point SAT holistic writing rubric as having the following values: An essay earning a score of 6 is categorized as outstanding writing that is "clear and consistent" with a few minor errors. The descriptors for a score of 6 use such terms as "well organized" with a "smooth progression of ideas" and a "variety of sentence structure" with "appropriate examples." The essay that would earn an SAT score of 5 would be "effective, demonstrating reasonably consistent mastery, although it will have occasional errors or lapses in quality" but is generally free of errors (SAT Scoring Guide, 2011 para. 2, 3).

Moving into the good to average range, an essay with a score of 4 is described as "competent, demonstrating adequate mastery, although it will have lapses in quality," while the essay represented by a score of 3 would be considered "inadequate, but demonstrates developing mastery" and would have weaknesses such as lacking variety or demonstrating poor sentence structure. An essay near the bottom with a score of 2 is "seriously limited, demonstrating little mastery, and is flawed by weaknesses in providing evidence, organization, focus, vocabulary, sentence structure, grammar or mechanics" (SAT Scoring Guide, 2011, para 4–5).

A score of 1 point is earned by an essay that demonstrates "very little or no mastery," with so many errors that the meaning is difficult to discern. A zero is reserved for the essay that is not written on the given assignment (SAT Scoring Guide, 2011, para 6–7).

The decisions on the essays are made by at least two SAT scorers, usually English teachers. They read each essay and score it according to the rubric. Scores that differ by more than 1 point are reassessed by a supervisor. Because the SAT essay is considered as a first draft, the scorers are instructed to overlook minor errors in spelling and grammar. Each scorer reads an average of 220 essays in 8 to 10 hours (Dobbs, 2005).Obviously, without the holistic rubric, the task of assessing the essays would be laborious and incredibly time consuming.

PERSUASIVE ESSAY PAPERS

Persuasive essays are often a requirement in AP courses. The holistic rubric below is an example that can be easily adapted to an analytic form with the addition of more categories such as *descriptive writing, research to support the position, sense of audience*, and so forth.

Holistic Rubric for a Persuasive Essay

(A score of zero is reserved for work not submitted or that is illegible or unintelligible)

4. The writer presents
   • deliberate and logical organization
   • many details and examples to support main ideas and to defend the position and addresses concerns and biases
   • a variety of sentence types (four or more)
   • a work that is error-free (spelling and mechanics)

3. The writer presents
   • logical organization
   • details and examples to support position and to address concerns and biases
   • at least three different types of sentences
   • a work that contains some errors (Errors do **not** interfere with the readers' understanding of the essay.)

2. The writer presents
   • little, if any logic to the organization
   • few details and/or examples to support position(may not address concerns or biases)
   • at least two different types of sentences
   • a work that contains several errors(Errors may interfere with the readers' understanding of the essay.)

1. The writer presents
   • no logical organization.
   • no details and/or examples

- no sentence variety
- a work that contains serious errors in spelling and mechanics (Errors interfere with the readers' understanding of the essay.) (California Department of Education, n.d.)

MATH RUBRICS

Math assessment methods at the high school level are comparable to methods used in the middle school. The middle school math rubric described in chapter 5, box 5.7 can be easily transferred for use with math students at the high school. Solutions and explanations as assessed and described with the middle school math rubric are still vital concepts of math assessment in these upper grades. However, in addition to solutions and explanations, the high school math teacher is also concerned with a student's understanding of concepts and procedures.

In the conceptual framework of mathematics, high school teachers often assess their student's ability to interpret the problem, to determine and discern what information is needed, and to apply the correct strategy for solution. Under the procedural component, a student's ability to demonstrate appropriate understanding of concepts, math terms, and strategies to solve and verify the answer is assessed (Bush, 2000).

The analytic math rubric to assess math concepts and procedures in box 6.4 can be compared to the generic 6-point holistic rubric in chapter 2, box 2.2

Box 6.4 Analytic Math Rubric (Concept and Procedure)

Math Concept

6. Exemplary conceptual understanding.
   - Full and detailed understanding of the concept.
   - The student uses all relevant information to solve the problem and can relate it to other situations.
   - Beyond expectations.

5. Commendable conceptual understanding.
   - Full understanding of the concept.
   - The student uses all relevant information to solve the problem.

4. Adequate conceptual understanding.
   - General understanding of the concept.

- The student determines the essential information but does not solve correctly.

3. Partial conceptual understanding.
   - The solution is not fully related to the question.
   - The student is unable to determine all the information needed to solve the problem.
   - The student is only partially able to make connections between/among the concepts.

2. Limited conceptual understanding.
   - The solution reveals little understanding of the concept and/or the solution is not related to the question.

1. Minimal conceptual understanding.
   - No understanding of the concept even though the problem was attempted.

0. No response; did not attempt to answer.

Math Procedure

6. Exemplary use of appropriate procedures.
   - Demonstrates full and detailed use of appropriate procedures with precise math terms and appropriate strategies to solve and verify the answer.
   - Beyond expectations.

5. Commendable use of appropriate procedures.
   - Full understanding of procedures and terms is evident.

4. Adequate use of appropriate procedures.
   - General understanding of procedures and terms with some confusion evident.

3. Partial use of appropriate procedures.
   - The student is not precise in using mathematical terms, principles, or procedures.
   - The student is partially able to carry out a procedure.

2. Limited use of appropriate procedures
   - The student has limited ability to use mathematical terms and principles and/or limited ability to carry out a procedure completely.

1. Minimal use of appropriate procedures.
   • Lacks use of appropriate procedures.
   • The student uses unsuitable methods to solve the math problem.

0. No response; did not attempt to answer.

Adapted with permission: T. Willenbrock, math teacher, Fairfax County Schools, Virginia.

If teachers are ranking work as high, medium, and low and are using the descriptors as listed in the math rubric in box 6.4, scores 6 and 5 would be considered high papers. The middle scores of 4 and 3 would be high-average and average, and the low scores of 2 and 1 would be attempts that need revisions or corrections. As always, the zero is reserved for the paper that is off task or not attempted.

RUBRICS FOR WORLD LANGUAGES IN HIGH SCHOOL

French, German, Spanish, Japanese–English-speaking students headed for college need to take a world language in their high school years. Because much of the assessment of language skills is performance-based, teachers of other languages often rely heavily on rubrics to assess the performance projects of their students. As one high school French teacher said, "I use them [rubrics] for all my projects. How would you score them without a rubric?"

Because the students' ability to speak and to write the language are two of her objectives, the French teacher has created projects and rubrics to evaluate these aspects of the language. The assignment illustrated in box 6.5 consists of having students call the teacher's work voice mail number and leave a message in French. This assignment can be adapted for other languages and is used to assess oral communication and the correct use of verb tense.

In addition to having the students leave a message, the teacher explained that her school voice mail is connected to her school e-mail, and she can actually play the messages through her laptop for the students to hear. "It's cool, because many times this is the first time they hear themselves speaking French." Listening to themselves gives them an opportunity to self-assess. Since giving students opportunities to self-assess connects back to the characteristics of resilient students and fair teachers, this project and its corresponding rubric meet the requirements for helping students to do their best.

Box 6.5 Rubric for Oral Assessment in French

TELEPHONEZ A LA PROF

Oral Verb Assessment

   To prove that you understand the use of the different verb tenses we have learned, I want you to do the following:

   This weekend you must call my school voice mail (xxx-xxx-xxxx ext. xxxx) and leave a message in French. Tell me the following:

• An appropriate greeting and your name
• Something you did over the weekend
• Something you are doing now
• Something you are going to do
• An appropriate good-bye
• Include one additional fact with each activity (e.g., what movie you are watching, with whom you went to the mall, etc.)

This is a graded assignment. Anyone not leaving a message by the time school begins on Monday will receive a zero.

You will be graded in the following way:

   Excellent—10 points: Includes all info, speaks without hesitation, uses correct pronunciation and grammar.

   Adequate—7 point: Missing some info, speaks with some hesitation, makes some errors in pronunciation and grammar.

   Unacceptable—1 point: Missing most info, speaks with much hesitation, many errors in pronunciation and grammar.

Source: Adapted with permission: Sue Whittaker, Norwin High School, North Huntingdon, Pennsylvania.

   Standardized assessment criteria for spoken languages can be used for students who are learning English as a second language as well as English-speaking students who are learning another tongue. A simple world language speaking criteria holistic rubric is often described as listed below.

World Language Speaking—Holistic Rubric

Task: Speaking in another language

4 points

• Student speaks on topic with ease and variety.

- Student can sustain a conversation with at least three interactions—one of which is student initiated.
- Pronunciation is not distracting.

3 points

- Student speaks on topic using at least three sentences.
- Student can answer at least two conversational questions.
- Pronunciation is partially distracting.

2 points

- Student provides short answers to speak on the topic or uses fewer than three sentences.
- Student unable to link words to complete thoughts.
- Student has difficulty in answering conversational questions.

1 point

- Student responds to questions with one word.
- Student's response is incomprehensible.
- Student uses native tongue for answers.

0 points

- Student makes no attempt to respond.

(S. Whittaker, Norwin School District, North Huntingdon, Pennsylvania, personal communication, May 18, 2011).

HOMEWORK RUBRICS

No discussion of assessment at the high school level would be complete without addressing homework. One of the reasons high school students give for not doing homework is because "it doesn't count" or "it's never graded." Another homework scenario as described by Sizer and Sizer (1999) is "bluffing" (pp. 39–57). Bluffing at the high school level involves not doing the assignment and hoping that it is not collected or that the "bluffer" never has to discuss the assignment in class. One way to counteract bluffing is to provide guidelines with the homework assignment.

The sample analytic homework rubric in Chapter 5 (box 5.2) will also work for high school students. However, the rubric below is a quickly-evaluated holistic rubric that would work at many grade levels.

Holistic Rubric for Homework in High School

4. Beyond expectations.

3. Complete
       Neat and easy to read
       Must have date and name
       Must be on time

2. Incomplete (directions not followed)
       Difficult to read
       Has name, missing the date
       May be on time

1. Partial
       Unorganized and/or difficult to read
       Missing name and date
       Late

0. Not submitted

SUMMARY

Using rubrics in high school can help to establish a sense of fairness and respect among students and teachers. Since students at this age are in jeopardy for dropping out of school, fostering an environment of mutual respect is crucial for developing educational resiliency and encouraging students to reach their full potential.

This chapter presented information on the developmental characteristics of young people in grades 9 through 12 with a glimpse of student advice to teachers. In addition, descriptions of the characteristics of successful high school teachers, resilient students, and some of the unique curriculum needs of these grades were discussed. Models of scoring rubrics appropriate for use in the high school grades for the assessment of group activities, oral presentations, world languages, written essays, math, and homework were provided.

REFERENCES

Aud, S., Hussar, W., Planty, M., Snyder, T., Bianco, K., Fox, M., Frohlich, L., Kemp, J., Drake, L. (2010). *The condition of education 2010* (NCES 2010–028). Washington, DC: National Center for Education Statistics, Institute of Education Sciences, U.S. Department of Education.

Bucher, K., and Manning, M. L. (2006).*Young adult literature: Exploration, evaluation, and appreciation.* Upper Saddle River, NJ: Pearson.

Bush, W. S. (2000). *Mathematics assessment: Cases and discussion questions for grades 6–12.* Reston, VA: National Council of Teachers of Mathematics.

California Department of Education (n.d.). High school exit examination: Response to writing prompt. Retrieved May 9, 2011 from score.rims.k12.ca.us/sub_standards/Scoring_Guide_Essay.html.

Cushman, K. (2003). *Fires in the bathroom: Advice for teachers from high school students.* New York: The New Press.

Dobbs, M. (January 15, 2005). Scorers of new SAT get ready for essays. *The Washington Post*, A1.

Feiler, R. and Tomonari, D. (2003). Child development: Stages of growth. *Encyclopedia of Education.* Retrieved May 7, 2011 from www.encyclopedia.com/doc/1G2–3403200106.html.

Grapevine-Colleyville Independent School District. (2002). *Curriculum guides. Developmental characteristics.* Retrieved February 23, 2005: www.gcisd-k12.org/lists/guides/ currguides_main.html.

Greene, J. P., and Foster, G. (2003). *Public high school graduation and college readiness rates in the United States.* New York: Center for Civic Innovation at the Manhattan Institute.

Huebner, T. A. and Corbett, G. C. (2005). *Rethinking high school: Five profiles of innovative models for student success.* Seattle, WA: Bill and Melinda Gates Foundation.

Jensen. E. (2005). *Teaching with the brain in mind.* 2ed. Alexandria, VA: ASCD.

Orfield, G., Losen, D., Wald, J., and Swanson, C. B. (2004). *Losing our future: How minority youth are being left behind by the graduation rate crisis.* Cambridge, MA: The Civil Rights Project at Harvard.

Paulsen, A. (2010, March 1). Obama pledges $900 million more to stem "dropout crisis." *Christian Science Monitor.* Retrieved March 20, 2011 from www.csmonitor.com/USA/ Education/2010/0301/Obama-pledges-900-million-more-to-stem-dropout-crisis.

SAT Scoring Guide (2011). Retrieved February 21, 2011 from www.collegeboard.com/student/ testing/sat/about/sat/essay_scoring.html.

SAT Writing Section (2011). Retrieved February 21, 2011 fromwww.collegeboard.com/ student/testing/sat/about/sat/writing.html.

Sizer, T. R., and Sizer, N. F. (1999). *The students are watching.* Boston: Beacon Press.

Topf, R. S., Frazier-Maiwald, V., and Krovetz, M. L. (2004). Developing resilient learning communities to close the achievement gap. In H. Waxman, Y. Padrón, and

J. Gray (Eds.), *Educational resiliency: Student, teacher, and school perspectives* (pp. 205–26).Greenwich, CT: Information Age Publishing.

Wang, M. C., Haertel, G. D., and Walberg, H. J. (1997). Fostering educational resilience in inner-city schools. *Children and Youth* (7), 119–40.

Wagoner, S. (2004). Developmental characteristics of youth: Implications for experiential learning. Retrieved April 4, 2011 from www.experientiallearning .ucdavis.edu/tlbx-ages.shtml.

Chapter 7

Rubrics with Adult Learners

Professors Are from Mars, Students Are from Snickers

—Ronald A. Berk

In choosing the above title for his book, *Professors Are from Mars, Students Are from Snickers*, Professor Ronald Berk (1998) has summed up the dynamic of teaching at the post–high school or college level. Teachers and their adult students often seem to come from different areas in the universe—or at least have different preferences for candy!

If professors and students appear to be from two different planets, it may be because the two cultures often seem to speak different languages. One area of frequent miscommunication is related to grades. Instructors and their adult students often differ in their views on the meaning or value of grades.

One answer to why their views on grading differ may be found in the studies of the adult learner. Authors often discuss the comparisons of adults and children as learners based on the cognitive and psychosocial stages of adults from the ages of 19 and beyond.

This chapter focuses on the differences between adults and children as learners; recent trends in grade inflation at the university level; the importance of grades for adult learners; and how using scoring rubrics with adult learners can help to address these issues.

THE ADULT LEARNER

Much has been written about theories of adult education or *andragogy* as opposed to *pedagogy*, which traditionally has been defined as the science of teaching without any age specification. The term *andragogy* was originated

Chapter 7

in 1833 by the German Alexander Kapp to describe Plato's discussion of adult education. The word can be contrasted to *pedagogy*, which has its 17th-century origins from the Greek prefix for child, *paes*, and the Greek verb, *agen* or *agogos*, to lead. Using the Greek prefix for man, *andr*, Kapp created *andragogy* to describe the science of teaching or leading adults (Knowles, 1990, 1980).

Erik Erikson, a human-development theorist, outlined the eight stages of life in his 1950 work, *Childhood and Society*. Each of the eight stages is developmental in nature and characterized by a descriptive conflict or psychological crisis. These eight stages, their corresponding age range, and conflicts are listed below. It is important to note that the conflicts are present throughout life, but are especially emphasized during the stage as indicated (Erikson, 1950; 1963).

Erikson's eight stages of life:

* Infancy (ages 0–1): Trust versus Mistrust
* Toddler (ages 1–2): Autonomy versus Shame and Doubt
* Early Childhood (ages 3–6): Initiative versus Guilt
* Middle Childhood (ages 6–12): Inferiority versus Industry
* Adolescence (ages 12–18): Identity versus Role Confusion
* Early Adulthood (ages 19–40): Intimacy versus Isolation
* Middle Adulthood (ages 40–65): Generativity versus Stagnation
* Late Adulthood (ages 65–death): Ego Integrity versus Despair (Erikson, 1950)

Based on these age ranges, the majority are the students in the postsecondary or college classrooms in the early adult stage and conflicted by intimacy and isolation, which means that they will either be able to form meaningful relations with others or remain self-absorbed. Some of our postsecondary students—especially those seeking a career change—are in Erikson's stage of middle adulthood where the crisis is whether they will have a sense of being a productive member of society or they will feel the stagnation of being unable to contribute.

A COMPARISON OF THE EMPHASIS
OF PEDAGOGY AND ANDRAGOGY

Adult education researcher, Malcolm Knowles (1980), listed five areas where the adult learner differs from the child learner. These areas of difference are:

1. Student self-concept
   • Pedagogy: Dependent on the teacher to direct the learning; moving to active learning.
   • Andragogy: Independent; able to self direct learning.

2. Student prior experiences
   • Pedagogy: Limited experience, but growing. Student shares teachers' experiences.
   • Andragogy: Often brings a wealth of life experience to the learning situation.

3. Student readiness to learn
   • Pedagogy: Ready to learn what society or the curriculum dictates. Learning is dependent on developmental stages.
   • Andragogy: Ready to learn what the individual needs for his or her perceived role.

4. Student application of learning
   • Pedagogy: Postponed application ("When will I use this?")
   • Andragogy: Immediate application ("How can I use this?")

5. Source of student motivation
   • Pedagogy: External
   • Andragogy: Intrinsic

(Dean, 2001; James, 1995; Knowles, 1980; Price, 1999; Webster, Zachariah, McFaury, and McMullin, 2001; Weil, 1986)

These areas, however, are not limited to either child or adult. For example, Knowles's first area of self-directed instruction is certainly not limited to adult learners. Active learning and the constructivist theory are current models for learning theory and acknowledge the need of all learners—children and adults—to construct their own knowledge with the teacher acting as the facilitator or guide.

A major area of difference between the child and adult learner is under the topic of experience. In the area of experience, the educators of adult students will be quick to recognize that, although their students do bring a wealth of prior experiences—including experience as a learner—into the classroom, these experiences may or may not be related to the subject being studied.

Although children view experience as something or an event that happens *to* them, adults often derive their identity or sense of importance from their experiences. Adult students are also more likely to feel rejected or unimportant if their experiences are ignored or are minimized. Because of this need for acknowledgment, adult educators are wise to include class time for their adult students to compare experiences.

While areas three and four (readiness and application) are self-explanatory, the fifth area of differences, motivation, is more complicated. Discussions with students at all levels about their motivations often reveal that motivation is closely related to grades—an extrinsic motivator—at both the adult and childhood stages of life. Although Knowles (1980) claims that motivation is more intrinsic at the adult level, a group of graduate students often place the grade earned above the knowledge gained, especially if financial reimbursement of tuition depends on the letter grade.

SUCCESSFUL TEACHERS OF ADULTS

Regardless of the motivation, Mark Tennant (1997) lists eight critical characteristics of successful teachers of adults. His recommendations are that teachers of adults should

- Value the experience of the learners.
- Engage in reflection of the learners' experiences.
- Establish the environment or spirit of a community of learners.
- Empower the students.
- Assess each student as an individual.
- Encourage learners to discuss conflicting points of view.
- Help students to identify the social, historical, and cultural bases for their experiences.
- Encourage a willingness to make changes based on learning experiences.

Using a well-crafted assessment rubric will help the educator of adults to address all eight critical characteristics, especially assessing each student as an individual.

GRADE INFLATION

Mention inflated grades to a group of college professors, and you will hear a variety of opinions based on their own prior experiences. Research conducted among the faculty at a liberal arts university revealed two related definitions of grade inflation.

The majority of the participants agreed that grade inflation is simply a change in the grading standard. That is, higher grades are awarded for the same level or quality of work that previously earned a lower grade. Others defined grade inflation as easy-grading or awarding higher grades than students earned (Barriga, Cooper, Gawelek, Butela, and Johnson, 2008).

Whatever the definition, research often contradicts itself concerning grade inflation. Some claim that college grade point averages have consistently increased since the Vietnam era, when not making the grade resulted in male students being drafted. Others claim that longitudinal studies reveal insignificant changes in college-level grade point averages through time.

Statistics on grade distribution in higher education published in 2002 from the U.S. Office of Education reveal that one half of all university students in the United States still earn a mixture of Bs, Cs and Ds, while about one-tenth earn a combination of As and Bs (U.S. Office of Education, 2002). A study conducted in 2010 verifies that that a slow rise in college-level GPAs has continued from 1980 until the present (Rojstaczer and Healy, 2010).

In the 1950s and 1960s, many educators at both high school and college levels "graded on the curve," which referred to a statistical bell curve. In the bell curve grading method, the smallest percent would earn As, and the same small percentage would earn Fs; the number of Bs would be matched by the number of Ds; and the largest percent (usually 68 percent are in the middle of a bell curve) would earn Cs.

In a move to combat grade inflation and move back to pseudo-curve grading, some universities have set a cap on the percentage of As that can be awarded in a course. Princeton University was the first to set a cap on the number of As earned at 35 percent per course (Mulvihill, 2005; Shoichet, 2002.) This means that no matter how well they perform in the course, 65 percent of the students may not earn an A in a course at that university.

ADULT STUDENTS AND GRADES

The conversation of a group of graduate students who were discussing the Princeton scenario revealed some insightful comments that provide support for the use of scoring rubrics in college. In defense of as many students as possible earning As, some participants argued that if the instructor at any level has clearly defined excellence or mastery (as in a rubric), it is possible for many more than 35 percent to earn As. Others stated that only the very best of any group should earn the highest scores. "If I do better work than the guy next to me, why do we both earn the same grade?"

Some comments even go back to the curve or continuum grading. As one high school teacher reminisced, "When I was in college, we used to joke that the professor just threw our papers down the stairs. The ones that landed on the top stairs were As and Bs; the bottom stairs were Ds and Fs, and all the rest were Cs." However, the summation quote may actually be when one student declared that the problem of so-called grade inflation might just be that professors do not put enough thought or time into refining their assessment criteria and tools.

USING SCORING RUBRICS AT THE COLLEGE LEVEL

The ultimate tool for refining assessment criteria is a well-defined scoring rubric. Students are aware that grading is often subjective in nature and that grades often reflect the bias of the evaluator. In addition, many students feel that "they have no control over the outcomes of their work and that nothing they can do will improve poor grades" (Holmes and Smith, 2003, p. 318).

However, as many college professors have learned, using the guidelines of a scoring rubric or a scoring sheet facilitates evaluation and provides a blueprint for both the grade-motivated and the knowledge-motivated student. In addition, many professors believe that scoring rubrics that accurately reflect course objectives are a prime solution to subjective grading. Using assessment tools such as analytic scoring rubrics that describe the mastery of content will help to combat grade inflation (Falkenberg, 1996).

Rubrics also help in assessing students as individuals, which is the fifth item of Tennant's (1997) characteristics of effective teachers of adults as listed above. As one veteran professor in the humanities said, "It is amazing that after 20 years we can still continue learning how to be more effective in our teaching! I have found over the years that the more specific I am about what I want from an assignment, the better the student work on the assignment will be. I have tried to learn each semester how to be more detailed in stating my expectations." The road to an A is clearly designated.

Although educators at all levels agree that knowledge is their business and grades are of less concern than the information or expertise that students gain, grading is still required. For the educator who prefers to focus on performance-based assignments, this emphasis on letter grades is often viewed as a necessary evil. A group of college professors who were willing to share experiences with scoring rubrics agreed that using scoring rubrics helped to remove subjectivity from performance-based assessment.

The head of a university drama department provided the unique class-participation self-assessment rubric illustrated box 7.1

Box 7.1 Individual Class Performance Self-Evaluation

Instructions: Rate yourself from 1 = low to 5 = high.

Attendance:

1. Attended classes and was on time and prepared

Small Group Involvement:

2. Applied knowledge gained from assignments to group activities
3. Showed interest in group discussions and activities
4. Was open-minded and listened to the comments of others
5. Helped facilitate group discussions
6. Asked questions of others
7. Helped group stay focused on tasks
8. Encouraged the participation of other group members

Class involvement:

9. Began classes with a positive and constructive attitude
10. Asked pertinent questions in class
11. Came prepared for class discussions
12. Brought assignments prepared for class
13. Articulated an understanding of class materials
14. Was able to respond effectively to questions posed by others
15. Took risks to stretch myself

Source: T. Brino-Dean, Theatre Department, Seton Hill University, Greensburg, Pennsylvania (personal communication, April 5, 2005).

He includes the rubric in the syllabus and then hands copies of the form out at the end of every three weeks of classes and has students do a self-evaluation of their in-class work. "I then take the form and look at my notes and determine a score for their class participation for that three-week period, write it on the form, and then return it to the students. I oftentimes point out areas for improvements by flagging parts of the form or writing notes to each student."

"There are a certain number of points that each student can earn for each class period, so they are building up and earning points as opposed to being penalized on some nebulous number of points or portion of their grade at the end of the semester. They get more consistent feedback this way, and it reminds them of what is expected in class.

"Obviously, if they miss class they miss the opportunity to earn the points from that class period, but I will give make-up assignments if they request them so that they can complete work that will help approximate what they missed from the class session to try to earn the points back. They get the message that what we do in class is important and valuable and that their participation is essential—and it actually puts a little pressure on me to make sure that classroom activities *are* in fact valuable! (T. Brino-Dean, personal communication , April 5, 2005)

Laptops and other mobile devices have prompted another professor to include this section on her analytic rubric for classroom participation:

- *Refrains from distracting behaviors, including non-class-related use of electronics:*

Outstanding	*Without exception.*
Very Good	*Almost always.*
Sufficient	*Engages in some distracting behaviors.*
Below expectations	*Disrupts the class more than occasionally.*

(C. Magistro, personal communication, May 24, 2011)

Instructors who rely on rubrics for assessing tend to become addicted to them. The rubric for assessing an oral presentation in box 7.2 came from a freshman course on thinking and writing taught by the same drama professor. His rubric is divided into content and presentation style.

Box 7.2 Oral Presentation Evaluation Rubric

Content: (40 possible points)

To what degree did the content of the presentation demonstrate the presenter's . . .

- Organization
  (structure, introduction, body, conclusion, easy to follow)

- Use of required elements
  (introduction, research question, findings/results, thesis, evidence supporting thesis, counterarguments)

- Information
  (value of information, relevance to topic, understanding of material)

- Visuals
(content and usage of tables, charts, posters, or displays)

Presentation Style: (60 possible points)

To what degree did the presentation style add or detract from the presentation?

- Volume
(spoke loudly enough; too loud)

- Clarity/Grammar
(spoke with good articulation/enunciation and correct grammar)

- Pace
(spoke too quickly, too slowly)

- Eye contact
(maintains eye contact with audience)

- Vocal Pauses/Crutches
(ahs, ums, you knows, ands, other)

- Body Control
(gestures, controlled movement, good posture, materials in order and not fumbled)

- Dynamic
(vocal variety—not monotone, comfort, humor, audience involvement)

- Time
(presented within the time frame)

- Visuals and/or handouts
(appropriateness, usefulness, appearance)

- Interest/Involvement of Audience
(invited questions, responded effectively to questions)

Comments:

Adapted with permission: T. Brino-Dean, Seton Hill University, Greensburg, Pennsylvania (personal communication, April 5, 2011).

He reported that "the oral presentation [rubric] is actually the one I use for [the class], but I change and adapt it depending on what the specific requirements of the presentation are." Although he has adjusted the point values (0–10 for the content and 0–6 for presentation style) to fit in with his assignment, he admits that the point values are easy to vary as the requirements change.

A professor in a university education division uses similar criteria for oral presentations of student lessons but adds "professionally presented" to her rubric. She explained, "I want them to realize that as future teachers, they must dress professionally for presentations. I tell them to dress in what they expect to wear to teach. It can be casual and comfortable, but not shorts, baseball caps, and flip flops."

This is echoed in the appearance section of an analytic rubric created by a professor in family and consumer sciences. Although the guide listed below was created for the teaching of lessons in elementary education, it is appropriate for any discipline where appearance is crucial.

RUBRIC TO EVALUATE PROFESSIONAL APPEARANCE

Appearance

- Exemplary—Professional appearance.
- Successful—Acceptable appearance.
- Fair—Appearance could be more polished.
- Not Yet—Appearance is inappropriate

Source: Doreen Tracy, Family and Consumer Sciences, Seton Hill University, Greensburg, Pennsylvania (personal communication, May 24, 2011)

RUBRICS FOR GRADING REFLECTION
PAPERS AND HOMEWORK

Many disciplines also use reflection as a crucial component. The rubrics illustrated below were created by a professor in the psychology department but could be used in a variety of courses for written assignments. She said, "Guidelines and checklists have made my life a lot easier. I know what to focus on when I'm reading student work, I'm less likely to feel helpless and overwhelmed, students are more satisfied because they can understand the strengths and shortcomings of their work, and I think my grading is less subject to whims, moods, and biases.

Guidelines for Grading Reflection Papers and Homework

I will assign a "5" to papers when all of the following apply:

1. The paper is well written, without errors.
2. When applicable, the paper integrates materials from two or more sources including, among other things, personal experience, various academic publications, assigned course readings, or lectures from other classes.
3. The paper presents a creative perspective or a creative analysis, one that reflects the writer's unique and focused thought.

I will assign a "4" to papers when

1. The paper includes no errors.
2. Points are clear, well organized, and persuasive.
3. The paper addresses the topic in depth or breadth, reflecting careful and thoughtful consideration of the topic at hand.

I assign an "3" to papers when

1. The paper is clearly written with zero to three errors in grammar, punctuation, and usage.
2. Ideas are organized into effective paragraphs.
3. The paper is accurate. Claims are supported by evidence, and opinions are identified as such. There are no errors.
4. The paper addresses each element of the assignment to some extent.

I will assign a "2" to papers when any of the following apply:

1. The paper is clearly written but has more than three errors in grammar, punctuation, and word usage.
2. The paper meets most of the requirements of the assignment but does not address one or more requirements adequately.
3. The paper is logically reasoned for the most part but includes some lapses in logic.

I will assign a "1" to papers when any of the following apply:

1. The paper largely ignores the questions or tasks assigned (e.g., the paper doesn't answer the questions posed or neglects an important directive.)
2. The paper is difficult to comprehend due to errors in language or usage.

3. The paper contains factual errors.
4. Paragraph or sentence organization is insufficient.

I will assign a "0" to papers when any of the following apply:

1. The paper is dishonest or plagiarized.
2. The paper is incomprehensible due to errors in language or usage.
3. Nothing was submitted.

(C. Magistro, psychology professor, Seton Hill University, Greensburg, Pennsylvania personal communication, May 5, 2005)

RESEARCH PAPERS

Research papers are customary assignments in many college courses. Two different approaches to evaluation of research papers are illustrated below.

The Research Paper Grading Form listed below divides the evaluation of the paper into three areas—format, technical, and content—and awards points in each area. Appropriately, the majority of the points are for content, but format and technical errors must also be addressed.

Research Paper Grading Form

FORMAT (possible 3 points each)

_____ Title
_____ Pagination
_____ Headings

TECHNICAL (possible 3 points each)

_____ Accurate grammar, punctuation, and word use
_____ Correct spelling, free from typos
_____ Mentioned attachments in the appropriate section in the text of the paper
_____ In-text citations present
_____ In-text citations correct
_____ Works cited correctly on works cited page
_____ Incorporated comments noted on previous draft

CONTENT (possible 10 points each)

_____ Introduction
_____ Research question/hypothesis

_____ Literature review (two articles from professional journals or reliable Internet sources, two books or chapters or essays from books; optional are articles from magazines and newspapers, and non-print media)
_____ Research method(s)
_____ Sampling
_____ Tables, charts or displays
_____ Works cited page

TOTAL POINTS OUT OF 100: _____

Please find summary comments on your paper, at the bottom of the last page of text.

(D. Droppa, professor, Social Work Program, Seton Hill University, Greensburg, Pennsylvania, personal communication, May 24, 2005)

Another research paper rubric example uses a subtraction method and actually deducts points from a possible total. A *minor* deduction could be two to three points from an 80-point-total paper. An *extreme* deduction on the same paper could subtract 12–15 points. Because he discusses this scoring system in detail with his students, it works for this instructor, but he admits, "I think it's only a rubric in the loose sense of the word."

Grading Sheet for Research Papers (Subtraction Method)

Deductions due to errors will be *Minor, Moderate, Major,* or *Extreme.* The range of deductions depends on the total value of the paper.

AREA: DEDUCTION:

APA format (including title and reference pages)   _____
Grammar and mechanics (intro and conclusion, proofread, no errors) _____
Paper Minimums (pages, style, and sources)   _____
Correct and Appropriate Content (answers thesis
question, good sources, etc.)   _____
Citations and Plagiarism [(possible failure if
Major; failure if *Extreme*) all parenthetical
documentation and sources present, cited sources
match reference page, absolutely no plagiarized information]   _____

TOTAL WORTH OF PAPER _____
TOTAL DEDUCTIONS _____
SCORE/GRADE _____

(E. Cooper, psychology professor, Seton Hill University, Greensburg, Pennsylvania personal communication, May23, 2011)

As brief as the subtraction-scoring sheet is, other rubrics spell out all possible details. The subjectivity of art assessment has been detailed into a rubric used in a design class. The art professor who designed the rubric presented below has been using this format with success "for many years."

Grading Rubric for Art Design Course

Design Investigations

- Concepts
    4. fully grasped
    3. minor inconsistencies
    2. considerable inconsistencies
    1. major inconsistencies
    0. no evidence of understanding

- Interpretation
    4. unique
    3. unusual
    2. familiar but effective
    1. visual cliché
    0. no attempt at individualization

- Craftsmanship
    4. flawless
    3. near flawless
    2. a few flaws but acceptable
    1. highly flawed, sloppy
    0. flawed to the point of unacceptable

Work Habits

4. always displays a positive attitude; speaks up quite often, a major contributor; frequently helps others
3. usually displays a positive attitude; speaks up often; a significant contributor; often helps others
2. consistency of attitude varies; speaks up on occasion, a minor contributor; rarely helps others
1. positive attitude rare; never speaks up, a non-contributor; never helps others
0. attitudinally dysfunctional; a non-contributor in all ways

Written Critiques/Observations

4. insightful; extensive; flawless grammar
3. insightful; extensive; near flawless grammar (1–2 errors)
2. some insight displayed; of minimum length; near flawless grammar (3–4 errors)
1. little insight; of less than minimum required length; frequent (5–7) errors of grammar
0. no insight; of less than minimum required length; excessive (more than 8) errors of grammar

(S. Thompson, Art Professor, Seton Hill University, Greensburg, Pennsylvania, personal communication, May 25, 2011).

A final support for using a type of rubric or scoring guide to assess the work of adult students came from a novice professor who had an adult student challenge the grade on a final project.

"When I met with [the student], I had the scoring rubric in hand, and we went over her individual project point by point." The student was immediately apologetic when she realized that she had omitted a component. Because the rubric had been distributed and was posted online, the student was forced to accept the responsibility for knowing the requirements. Other instructors agreed that they had fewer students question their grades when they had a rubric for reference.

SUMMARY

Instructors and college students often differ in their views on the meaning or value of grades. For the faculty member, grades primarily serve as evaluations of the abilities of their students based on the quality of their work. For students, grades can be a motivation for studying and attending class. If students are grade-motivated, the grade and the credits earned toward the degree are their primary aims of the course; however, for those students who are learning-motivated, the grades are of less concern than the information or expertise they gain.

One of the main differences in teaching to a classroom of adults when compared to students in grades K–12 is the recognition that these adult students bring with them a variety of life experiences upon which the instructor can build. These experiences often include prior grading experiences—both positive and negative. Using rubrics with adult learners helps to address issues of fairness in grading subjective assignments, assessing each assignment as an individual work, and providing a picture of what excellence in each assignment resembles.

This chapter concentrated on the unique learning needs of the adult student, the differences between adults and children as learners, the assessment and grading of adult assignments, recent trends in grade inflation at the university level, and how using scoring rubrics with adult learners can help to address these issues. Sample grading scenarios and scoring rubrics were provided.

REFERENCES

Barriga, A. Q., Cooper, E. K., Gawelek, M. A., Butela, K., and Johnson, E. (2008). Dialogue and exchange of information about grade inflation can counteract its effects. *College Teaching,* 56(4), 201–209.

Berk, R. A. (1998). *Professors are from Mars, students are from Snickers.* Madison, WI: Mendota Press.

Dean, G. J. (2001). Why do adult educators educate adults? In T. Reiff and E. McDevitt (Eds.), *Pennsylvania ABLE Staff Handbook.* Retrieved April 27, 2005: www.able.state.pa.us/able.

Erikson, E. H. (1950). *Childhood and society.* New York: W. W. Norton and Company.

Erikson, E. H. (1963). *Childhood and society.* (2nd ed.). New York: W. W. Norton and Company.

Falkenberg, S. (1996). Grade inflation. Retrieved March 26, 2011, people.eku.edu/falkenbergs/grdinfla.htm.

Holmes, L. E., and Smith, L. J. (2003). Student evaluations of faculty grading methods. *Journal of education for business*, 78(6), 318–23.

James, D. (1995). Mature studentship in higher education: Beyond a species approach. *British Journal of Sociology of Education*, 16(4), 451–65.

Knowles, M.S. (1990) *The adult learner. A neglected species, 4th Edition.* Houston, TX: Gulf.

Knowles, M.S. (1980). *The modern practice of adult education: From pedagogy to andragogy.* (Rev. ed.). New York: Association Press.

Mulvihill, G. (2005, January 23). Princeton students on edge over A's. *Greensburg Tribune Review*, p. A5.

Rojstaczer, S. and Healy, C. (2010). Grading in American colleges and universities. *Teachers College Record.* Retrieved March 24, 2011: www.gradeinflation.com/tcr2010grading.pdf.

Price, D. W. (1999). Philosophy and the adult educator. *Adult Learning,* 11(2), 3–5.

Shoichet, C. (2002, July 12). Reports of grade inflation may be inflated, study finds. *Chronicle of Higher Education*, 48(44), A37.

Tennant, M. (1997). *Psychology and adult learning* (2nd ed.). New York: Routledge.

U.S. Office of Education. (2002). *Profiles of U.S. post-secondary education institutions: 1999–2000*. Washington, DC: Author.

Webster K., Zachariah, M., McFaury, J. and McMullin, L. (2001). Do adults and children learn differently? *Questions and Answers on Adult Education*. Retrieved May 27, 2005: fcis.oise.utoronto.ca/~daniel_schugurensky/faqs/qa9.html.

Weil, S. (1986). Nontraditional learners within traditional higher education institutions: Discovery and disappointment. *Studies in Higher Education*, 11, 219–35.

Chapter 8

Using Rubrics with Students Who Have Special Needs

The pessimist complains about the wind; the optimist expects it to change; the realist adjusts the sails.

—William Arthur Ward

Teachers of students with special needs are realistic experts in "adjusting the sails." These dedicated professionals know that their students will succeed with the proper adjustment. Often, the dilemma is where to find that perfect adjustment. A professor of special education is known to tell her students, "good teaching is simply good teaching."

The same excellent teaching strategies that work in the general education classroom will also work with students with special needs. Differentiated instruction—making adjustments and adaptations to curricula to begin where each student is and moving from that point—is advised for teachers of typical and atypical students alike. What often separates the special education teacher from the regular education teacher is the mountain of legalities and paperwork requiring assessments and evaluations. Checklists (see chapter 2) and rubrics can help to simplify the process. This chapter defines special needs, provides evidence supporting the use of rubrics with students with special needs, and includes sample rubrics used in special education settings.

DEFINITIONS OF SPECIAL NEEDS

Experienced teachers of students with special needs often cannot agree on a definition. One definition, based on the U.S. Department of Education, states, "Special needs have generally been identified through the Individuals with Disabilities Education Act. Young children who have been diagnosed as having developmental delays, or any child who has been evaluated as having one of a limited list of disabilities specified in IDEA [*See Box 8. 1 for the limited list of disabilities*] are considered as having special needs when they require special education and related services" (Brennan and Rosenzweig, 2008, para.1; U.S. Department of Education, 2007).

Nearly 7 million children with disabilities receive special education services under IDEA, including 270,000 infants and toddlers, 715,000 preschool-age children, and 6 million students from ages 6 through 21" (Brennan and Rosenzweig, 2008, para.1; U.S. Department of Education, 2007).

A more simple definition of special needs states that, "Students with special needs are those who require instructional adaptations in order to learn successfully" (Lewis and Doorlad, 2011, p. 4). This simple definition does not equate special needs with disability; therefore, it includes students identified as "gifted." When defining special needs, it should be noted that *Rosa's Law* became effective in 2010 and mandates that Federal statutes will use the less offensive phrase "intellectual disability" to describe the formerly used "mental retardation" (Sweet, 2010).

Box 8.1 Special Needs Conditions as Listed in IDEA

1. Autism—developmental disability significantly affecting verbal and nonverbal communication and social interaction, generally evident before age three.
2. Deaf-Blindness—simultaneous hearing and visual impairments
3. Deafness
4. Developmental Delay—a delay in a delay in one or more of the following areas: physical development; cognitive development; communication; social or emotional development; or behavioral development. *NOTE: On some lists, this category is omitted.*
5. Emotional Disturbance—one or more of the following:
   (a) An inability to learn that cannot be explained by intellectual, sensory, or health factors.
   (b) An inability to build or maintain satisfactory interpersonal relationships with peers and teachers.
   (c) Inappropriate types of behavior or feelings under normal circumstances.
   (d) A general pervasive mood of unhappiness or depression.
   (e) A tendency to develop physical symptoms or fears associated with personal or school problems.

6. Hearing Impairment
7. Intellectual Disability
8. Multiple Disabilities
9. Orthopedic Impairment
10. Other Health Impairment—having limited strength, vitality, or alertness, including a heightened alertness to environmental stimuli, that results in limited alertness with respect to the educational environment that is due to chronic or acute health problems such as asthma, attention deficit disorder or attention deficit hyperactivity disorder, diabetes, epilepsy, a heart condition, hemophilia, lead poisoning, leukemia, nephritis, rheumatic fever, sickle cell anemia, and Tourette syndrome.
11. Specific Learning Disability—a disorder in one or more of the basic psychological processes involved in understanding or in using language, spoken or written, that may manifest itself in the imperfect ability to listen, think, speak, read, write, spell, or to do mathematical calculations. The term includes such conditions as perceptual disabilities, brain injury, minimal brain dysfunction, dyslexia, and developmental aphasia.
12. Speech or Language Impairment
13. Traumatic Brain Injury
14. Visual Impairment Including Blindness

Source: NICHCY, n.d.

SPECIAL EDUCATION SITUATIONS THAT BENEFIT FROM RUBRICS

As one special education teacher noted, "Ideally, assessment should be a learning experience, not just grades. Rubrics that provide detailed descriptors can help all students. However, students with special needs especially benefit from knowing what the good one looks like."

One of the main differences in rubrics for students with special needs is that the rubric is often created for the *individual* as opposed to the entire class. However, many whole-class assignment rubrics can be adapted for the individual without drawing attention to the differences. In addition to classroom assignments, rubrics can be used to assess the required elements of the special education program. These include the Individualized Education Program and the Response to Intervention (IEPs and RtIs).

INDIVIDUALIZED EDUCATION PROGRAM (IEP)

Since 1974's Education for All Children Act, the Individualized Education Program (IEP) has become a part of *all s*pecial education annual team planning including students identified as gifted and talented. (The individualized program for a student identified as "gifted" is known as a GIEP.) The planning team, which includes educators, parents, and child where appropriate, creates a document that includes eight required elements and must be approved by and signed by parents: These eight elements of an IEP include:

- Present levels of educational and social performance where appropriate. This is based on observations, test results, and special education evaluations.
- Measurable annual goals that include either benchmarks or short-term objectives.
- Description of how the progress on annual goals will be assessed.
- The required special education and related services.
- The extent the student will participate in general education and a rationale for any non-participation.
- Modifications and accommodations that will be made to the general education environment, including the use of local and state tests.
- Dates and frequency of services.
- A statement of transition to post-secondary life (by age 16). (Lewis and Doorlag, 2011; Logston, n.d.)

RESPONSE TO INTERVENTION (RtI)

RtI is a model of instruction promoted in the regulations that accompanied the 2004 reauthorization of the federal Individuals with Disabilities Education Act. It blends the general and special education resources. It provides for three tiers or levels of intensity of instruction:

Tier One—"Universal" tier—instruction and services are available to **all** students—(ex: tutoring centers; differentiated instruction in the classroom).

Tier Two—Targeted, short-term instruction for **some** students who need more help to master a subject.

Tier Three—Intensive—Possibly needs special education services for relatively **few** students.

Progress in all tiers is monitored with short assessments (Samuels, 2009).

IEPS, RtIS, AND RUBRICS

A veteran special education teacher once said. "The ideal situation is when the assessment process is also a learning process. Presenting a rubric to my special-needs students helps them to gauge exactly what they will need to do." Especially helpful in addressing IEP goals, analytic rubrics can focus all of the following recommended strategies.

- Break assignments into segments of shorter tasks or steps, monitoring and evaluating each step
- Explain learning expectations to the student.
- Provide models of the end product.
- Provide written and verbal direction with visuals if possible.
- Break long assignments into small sequential steps, monitoring each step.
- Highlight key points within the written direction of the assignment.
- Grade spelling separately from content. (Webster, 2008)

Other recommendations for the assessment of students with special needs in both the general and special classrooms can be addressed with well-designed rubrics. These recommendations include:

- *The student should be involved in the assessment design.* (See chapter 11 on student-generated rubrics.) Although students participate in planning some aspects of the assessment, ultimately the classroom teacher decides how to implement the assessment. There are always some aspects in any rubric that are nonnegotiable.
- *The assessment tool should provide constructive information for all members of the child's IEP team*—the teachers, the students, and the parents. When used to identify strengths and weaknesses, rubrics provide needed data to support educational decisions. (Markusic, 2009)

The rubrics may be used in the general or special education classroom or even for progress in various therapy sessions. It is important to note that the special education rubric that measures IEP progress can be used to assess that progress in multiple environments and situations. Some district-wide rubrics are included on students' IEPs as a required assessment venue.

When creating rubrics for IEPs or for academic achievement, it is crucial to make the areas manageable for students. Setting students up for failure can be a concern in all classrooms (Bethlehem Central School District, 2007; Makusic, 2009).

Because rubrics are a way to provide assessment data for skills or behaviors that can be difficult to measure, they can be used for observation of a student's performance and behavior in a variety of settings and times. For example, the visual perception rubric illustrated in Box 8.2 is an example of a rubric that clearly describes situations for student discernment.

BOX 8.2 Visual Perception Rubric

Scoring Guide
1 Skill not displayed in any setting (even with support given)
2 Skill displayed erratically with models/prompts.
3 Skill displayed reliably with models/prompts
4 Skill displayed unaided

Spatial Relationships
_____ Perceives the positions of objects in relation to self
_____ Can complete up to 5-piece jigsaw puzzle
_____ Can complete up to 10-piece jigsaw puzzle

Visual Discernment
_____ Distinguishes shapes
_____ Discriminates positions
_____ Differentiates colors
_____ Distinguishes size

Visual Memory
_____ Remembers features of an item (shape, texture, color, size)
_____ Remembers order of seven items

Adapted from Bethlehem School District, 2007; Callandar and Buttris, 2008; Teaching Expertise, n.d.

Social communication skills are frequently a goal of an IEP. For the social skills rubric in Box 8.3, the evaluator observes the student in a social situation and uses the rubric to note the student' s performance level in initiating a topic, taking turns, and so on.

If the evaluators observe a weakness in an area not listed, they can easily add it to the rubric. The scoring guide calls for an observer to carefully monitor and rate the student's behavior in a variety of social situations. However, this rubric could also be used simply as a checklist to determine skills that need concentrated effort.

Box 8.3 Social Skills in Primary Grades

Scoring Guide

0—Skill not observed

1—Skill rarely observed—fewer than once per day

2—Skill occasionally observed—at least once per day

3—Skill usually observed—observed more than once daily

4—Skill consistently observed—never forgets

Conversational Skills

_____ Uses greetings appropriately

_____ Understands and uses appropriate body language

_____ Initiates, maintains, and appropriately ends conversations

_____ Uses appropriate turn-taking

_____ Maintains appropriate physical distance

_____ Uses appropriate volume, tone, and rate

_____ Avoids topics that upset others

_____ Asks permission

_____ Expresses needs

_____ Asks questions

_____ Active listening skills during brief conversation

_____ Plans before speaking

Social Skills Behavior

_____ Follows simple game rules

_____ Shows appropriate sportsmanship

_____ Does not display unusual sounds and/or behaviors

_____ Accepts peers' differences and mistakes

_____ Respects others' personal space

_____ Responds to touch appropriately

Socially Responsible Behavior

_____ Demonstrates appropriate play behaviors

_____ Invites peer to play

_____ Asks to join in ongoing play

_____ Engages in play for short time

_____ Demonstrates ability to share

_____ Respects rights and property of others

_____ Recognizes authority and follows instructions

_____ Demonstrates appropriate behavior in variety of settings

_____ Asks for help appropriately

_____ Is able to problem solve in social situations
_____ Manages external and internal distractions

Personal Presentation / Hygiene
_____ Wears appropriate clothing
_____ Manages cleanliness
_____ Uses appropriate table manners
_____ Personal health care (covering mouth when coughing, uses tissues, etc.)

Adapted from Bethlehem School District, 2007; Callandar and Buttris, 2008; Stormont, Espinosa, Knipping, and McCathren, 2003.

A similar high school rubric for social skills uses many of the skills as listed in Box 8.3. However, because the goal is to have the student assimilate into the general population, it uses the following scoring guide:

- 0. The skill is not observed even with coaching.
- 1. The student is unable to experience small social environments, but the skill is observed with coaching.
- 2. The skill is developing, but the student would still need coaching to move to a general classroom or to a job.
- 3. The skill is consistent in the small environment, but still might need coaching in a larger environment. Possibly hirable.
- 4. The top score of four is reserved for when the skill is comparable to the general population.(Bethlehem School District, 2007)

DAILY TASK AND INDIVIDUAL RUBRICS

Since special education rubrics often involve behavior, many teachers use a rubric that lists the days of the week across the top with daily tasks along the left side. Although this can be used with numerical values, it can also function as a checklist or even a sticker reward chart. Wise teachers begin with one or two tasks and gradually increase the list often limiting the numbers of general tasks to fewer than six to make the list manageable for both student and teacher. Although these rubrics are individually prepared, some general tasks often include on a daily rubric are:

- Stays in seat for class time
- Keeps hands and feet to self
- Follows directions

- Writes name as directed
- Responds appropriately

RUBRICS IN ACADEMIC AREAS

Individual rubrics can also be created in academic areas. A special education teacher of second graders often creates individual rubrics for future assessments right on the back of the student's paper. "I realize what I need to focus on as I see the student's errors and strengths, so I just flip the paper over and make notes. Of course, I need to remember to make a copy of that [paper] before I return the paper to be taken home. I use a double checkmark on the front as a signal for myself to double-check the reverse side before returning it." She added that the notes on the reverse side of the student paper can also provide a basis for conferencing with students and parents.

A fourth-grade teacher of students with special needs relates, "I use [rubrics] quite a bit in the classroom for science or reading projects, but also in writing. I typically create them myself on the computer, based on what requirements I have for the project and what I want the students to focus on: skills, content, etc." (D. Brino-Dean, personal communication, April 8, 2005).

Because students with special needs are often included in the state assessment tests, writing rubrics are often used at all levels. A high school teacher of students with special needs provided the essay rubric in Box 8.4. She said the rubric is used by all learning support teachers at the high-school level. While this rubric is specified for special education use, it is comparable to those used in the general education classrooms.

It is an excellent example of a tool that students and parents can also use to self-assess.

BOX 8. 4 High School Learning Support Essay Rubric—50 Possible Points

CATEGORY	POSSIBLE POINTS
A. Introduction (4–6 sentences)	**8 possible total points**
• Does the introduction catch the reader's attention? (Style)	2
• Is the introductory paragraph well developed? (Background info)	2

- Does the introduction include a clear   4
  thesis statement? (Focus)

B. Body (7–10 sentences each)   **14 possible total points**

- Does each body paragraph contain a   3
  clear topic sentence? (Focus)
- Does each body paragraph follow   3
  in the order in which it was presented in the
  thesis sentence? (Organization)
- Does the body have 3–5 examples or   4
  details to support the topic sentence?
  (Content Development)
- Are the examples or details adequately   4
  developed? (Content Development)

C. Conclusion(2–3 sentences)   **8 possible total points**

- Does the conclusion contain a   4
  reminder of the thesis sentence? (Style)
- Does the conclusion contain a summary   4
  statement? (Style)

D. Mechanics and Style   **10 possible total points**

- Is the paper free of errors in usage and   6
  mechanics? (Conventions)
- Are all sentences clear and varied in   4
  length and structure? (Style)

E. Writing Process   **10 possible total points**

- Is there a neat final draft?   3
- Is there a hand-written rough draft?   3
- Is there a typed rough draft with peer   4
  editing corrections?

TOTAL POSSIBLE POINTS—50

Source: K. Haile, Learning Support Teacher, Hempfield Area High School, Hempfield, Pennsylvania

Although the above essay rubric is used in a full-time learning support high school classroom, the format is easily adapted for the student with special needs who is included in the general education class.

RUBRICS IN GIFTED EDUCATION

Opponents of rubrics contend that rubrics stifle creativity, especially in gifted students. They argue that students will submit only the minimum for the A points. However, teachers of gifted students recognize that a well-constructed rubric that provides a top score for work "beyond expectations" actually encourages creativity. In addition, the rubric blueprint helps the frequent perfectionist gifted students to achieve their best work without undue stress (Cline and Schwartz, 1998; Karnes and Stephens, 2008; Winebrenner, 2001).

Tasks that are at the higher levels of Bloom's Taxonomy are appropriate to use for rubric creation for students identified as gifted. Some verbs used as descriptors for these higher level tasks include: *differentiates, applies, creates, revises,* and *generalizes. (*See Box 2.1 for a complete listing of Bloom's Taxonomy, General Objectives, and Verbs.)

For example, an analytic rubric to assess critical thinking used in Hawaii Public Schools has the following four areas:

- Applies prior learning experiences to new situations [*generalizes*]
- Considers multiple perspectives [*differentiates*] in analyzing and solving a variety of problems
- Generates [*creates*] new and creative ideas and approaches to developing solutions
- Evaluates the effectiveness and ethical considerations of a solution and makes adjustments [*revises*] as needed.

The four grading score areas range from
>*Consistently (4)*
>*Usually (3)*
>*Sometimes (2)*
>*Rarely (1)*
>*Never (0)* (Hawaii Public Schools, n.d.)

As with most parents, parents of students identified as gifted appreciate the clarity and purpose that rubrics provide. As one parent commented after being shown the critical thinking rubric, "Well, that certainly helps to clarify what they [teachers] mean by 'critical thinker' in grade five. This will eliminate many tears—from both of us."

SUMMARY

Typical and atypical students alike benefit from the feedback provided by scoring rubrics. Students identified as gifted, as well as pupils with severe developmental delays, demonstrate progress when rubrics explain the assessment. Assessing progress on IEPs and other required special education credentials can be simplified by a well-constructed rubric. These individually-created rubrics provide documentation for all stakeholders including parents.

This chapter has provided definitions of special needs, provided evidence supporting the use of rubrics with students with special needs, and included sample rubrics.

REFERENCES

Bethlehem Central School District. (2007). Special education. Retrieved April 1, 2011 from bcsd.k12.ny.us/specialeducation/rubrics.html.

Brennan, E.M, and Rosenzweig, J.M. (2008, May). *Parents of children with disabilities and work-life challenges: Presentation summary.* Presented at the Alfred P. Sloan Work and Family Research Network Panel Meeting, Chestnut Hill, MA. Retrieved April 2, 2011 from: wfnetwork.bc.edu/glossary_entry .php?term=Special%20Needs.%20Definition(s)%20ofandarea=All.

Callandar, A. and Buttris, J. (2008). *A–Z of special needs for every teacher.* London, UK: Optimus.

Cline, S. and Schwartz, D. (1998). *Diverse populations of gifted children: Meeting their needs in the regular classroom and beyond.* Upper Saddle River, NJ: Merrill/ Prentice-Hall.

Hawaii Public Schools (n.d.). General learner outcomes. GLO 3 complex thinker. Retrieved May 26, 2011: doe.k12.hi.us/curriculum/GLO_rubric_grade1–6.htm.

Karnes, F. A. and Stephens, K. R. (2008). *Achieving excellence: Educating the gifted and talented.* Upper Saddle River, NJ: Merrill/Prentice-Hall.

Lewis, R.B. and Doorlag, D. H. (2011). *Teaching students with special needs in general education classrooms,* 8ed. Upper Saddle River, NJ: Pearson.

Logston, A. (.n.d.). Top 8 essential parts of an individual education program. *About.com Guide.* Retrieved April 1, 2011 learningdisabilities.about.com/od/ publicschoolprograms/ tp/partsofaniep.htm.

Markusic, M. (2009). Characteristics of good classroom assessment. *Bright Hub.* Retrieved April 1, 2011 from www.brighthub.com/education/special/articles/5480 .aspx.

National Dissemination Center for Children with Disabilities (NICHCY) (n.d.). Categories of disabilities under IDEA law. Retrieved March 31, 2011: www .nichcy.org/disabilities/ categories/pages/default.aspx.

Samuels, C.A. (2009). High schools try out RTI. *Education Week.* Retrieved January 28, 2009 from www.edweek.org/ew/articles/2009/01/28/19rti_ep.h28 .html?print=1.

Stormont, M., Espinosa, L., Knipping, N. and McCathren, R. (2003). Supporting vulnerable learners in the primary grades: Strategies to prevent early school failure. *Early Childhood Research and Practice* 5(2). Retrieved May 19, 2011: ecrp.uiuc .edu/v5n2/stormont.html.

Sweet, L. (2010). Obama signs "Rosa's law." *The scoop from Washington.* Retrieved March 31, 2011 from blogs.suntimes.com/sweet/2010/10/obama_signs_rosas_ law_mental_r.html.

Teaching Expertise (n.d.). Activities to develop visual perception. Retrieved May 19, 2011: www.teachingexpertise.com/articles/activities-to-develop-visual-perception-1107.

U.S. Department of Education. (2007). Children with disabilities receiving special education under Part B of the Individuals with Disabilities Education Act. Office of Special Education Programs, Data Analysis System (DANS), OMB #1820–0043. Retrieved March 29, 2011 from: www.ideadata.org/arc_toc8.asp#partb.

Webster, J. (2008). Practical strategies for the classroom: Strategies for special education.*About.com Guide.* Retrieved April 1, 2011from specialed.about .com/cs/teacherstrategies/a/Strategies.htm.

Winebrenner, S. (2001). *Teaching gifted kids in the regular classroom: Strategies and techniques every teacher can use to meet the academic needs of the gifted and talented.* Minneapolis, MN: Free Spirit.

Chapter 9

Rubrics to Assess Educational Technology

> The farther backward you can look, the farther forward you are likely to see.
>
> —Winston Churchill

Churchill, in the above quote, was obviously being kind to those of us who are now known as "digital immigrants." For teachers who can look backward before the introduction of personal computers, the concept of assessing technology in education is relatively new territory.

However, in order to assess technology, one must accept that it is here to stay. As one novice teacher described her veteran teaching partner, "Although we get along well, Mrs. G. and I have divergent views on almost everything in the classroom! For example, I love technology and go to great lengths to incorporate it into classroom activities. Mrs. G's favorite quote is, 'A piece of chalk never malfunctions.'"

Although educators can see the humor in Mrs. G's chalk analogy, they also know that to ignore the values of technology in education is to ignore the importance of technology in their students' futures. And along with the recognition of the importance of technology in education comes the need to evaluate and assess.

Educational assessment in technology falls into two broad categories: assessing assignments that use technology and evaluating technology resources. Teachers need to evaluate assignments such as essays, blogs, and presentations that have been assigned—either in face-to-face or online courses. In addition, students and teachers need to evaluate software, Internet sites, and applications that are part of the current rage and the current curriculum. This chapter provides background information and sample rubrics for both technology assessment areas.

BACKGROUND

In 1995, about 12 percent of adults in the United States were connected to the Internet. In 2004, that number had grown to about 65 percent of American adults on line (Pew Internet and American Life Project, 2005). By 2009, surveys reveal that over 80 percent of homes in the United States have computers and 90 percent of those have Internet access (Neilson, 2009). It is not surprising that preschoolers are as comfortable with "drag and click" as they are with their "sippy cups." The term "digital natives" applies to these young people who have been familiar with computers from early childhood. Because most teachers today have not always had computers as tools ("digital immigrants"), they often learn from their students (Prensky, 2001).

COMPUTERS IN SCHOOLS

In addition to computer labs with banks of 20–25 computers, some schools have pods of computers in each classroom that are used for a variety of projects including word-processing, research, and games to enhance learning. Some schools are providing laptops or other Internet-connected mobile devices for teachers and students.

Teachers are finding creative ways to adapt to the changes. One teacher related, "The students in my high school classroom must place their cell phones and iPods in a basket on my desk on a daily basis. If they do this for two weeks, they are rewarded with a free period and snacks . . . and they respond in a positive way."

Attendance, memos, grades, and other requirements of classroom management are now communicated to the central office from the computer on the teacher's desk making the job of the elementary classroom "messenger" obsolete in some schools!

TECHNOLOGY CURRICULA

Along with computers in schools comes the need for standards and courses of study. The International Society for Technology in Education (ISTE) has provided lists of standards for teachers, administrators, and students. All three sets of standards are designed to provide "teachers, technology planners, teacher preparation institutions, and educational decision-makers with frameworks and standards to guide them in establishing enriched learning environments supported by technology" (ISTE/NETS, n.d., p. 1). The NETS (National Education Technology Standards) are not subject-matter specific, but rather are listings of technology skills required for students to have the expertise required to compete in a global arena.

The following recommended experiences with technology and digital resources are examples of learning activities in which students might engage during PK–Grade 2 (ages 4–8):

- Illustrate and communicate original ideas and stories using digital tools and media-rich resources.
- Identify, research, and collect data on an environmental issue using digital resources and propose a developmentally appropriate solution.
- Engage in learning activities with learners from multiple cultures through e-mail and other electronic means.
- In a collaborative work group, use a variety of technologies to produce a digital presentation or product in a curriculum area.
- Find and evaluate information related to a current or historical person or event using digital resources.
- Demonstrate safe and cooperative use of technology.
- Independently apply digital tools and resources to address a variety of tasks and problems.
- Communicate about technology using developmentally appropriate and accurate terminology.
- Demonstrate the ability to navigate in virtual environments such as electronic books, simulation software, and websites. (IST-NETS-S, 2011)

These activities can easily be converted to checklists and rubrics for assessment purposes. By doing so, teachers will easily meet the ISTE assessment requirement to "provide students with multiple and varied formative and summative assessments aligned with content and technology standards and use resulting data to inform learning and teaching" (NETS-T, 2011, para.2, d). Because scoring rubrics are both *formative* (helps the learner to improve) and *summative* (a final evaluation) in nature, they easily meet technology assessment requirements. A complete listing of NETS for teachers can be found at www.iste.org/standards/nets-for-teachers/nets-for-teachers-2008.aspx.

DIGITAL-AGE LEARNING ASSESSMENTS

Teachers today must not only design and develop authentic learning experiences using technology; they must also create appropriate assessments to support these experiences. Three of the National Educational Technology Standards for Teachers (NETS-T) are listed below.

Teachers are required to:

- Develop technology-enriched learning environments that enable all students to pursue their individual curiosities and become active participants in setting their own educational goals, managing their own learning, and assessing their own progress,
- Customize and personalize learning activities to address students' diverse learning styles, working strategies, and abilities using digital tools and resources, and
- Provide students with multiple and varied formative and summative assessments aligned with content and technology standards and use resulting data to inform learning and teaching. (ISTE-NETS-T, 2011)

Because scoring rubrics are easily adapted to meet individual objectives, creating rubrics will help educators meet the three assessment standards of *student self-assessment*, *individual and personalized assessment*, and *formative and summative evaluations*.

A computer teacher uses the self-assessment rubric below. This teacher created a poster of this rubric to hang in the lab and occasionally has students informally assess themselves before the end of the class period. A classroom teacher noted that students actually remind each other about bringing needed materials as they are lining up for computer class. The rubric has provided an awareness of the requirements and has helped students to focus on the task at hand.

COMPUTER LAB SELF-ASSESSMENT RUBRIC

HOW GOOD IS YOUR WORK?

3. This is better than my best work. I am very proud of this.
2. This is my best work. I am proud of this.
1. I can do better. This is not my best work.
0. I did not hand in any work.

HOW DID YOU USE YOUR TIME?

3. I used every minute on my work. OR My work was handed in before it was due.
2. I used most—but not all—of the time on my work. OR My work was handed in when it was due.
1. I goofed off for most of the class. OR My work was late.
0. I goofed off for the entire class. OR I did not hand in my work at all.

HOW MUCH DO YOU UNDERSTAND?

3. I understand all the computer steps and terms and have no questions. I can always help others.
2. I understand most of the computer steps and terms and have one or two questions. I can sometimes help others.
1. I understand some of the computer steps and terms, but I need help lots of times.
0. I do not understand what we are doing. I need help all of the time.

DID YOU BRING THE RIGHT MATERIALS?

3. I always bring the right materials to class.
2. I almost always bring the right materials to class.
1. I sometimes bring the right materials to class.
0. I always forget to bring the right materials to class.

HOW DID YOU ACT?

3. I am always ready to listen and to begin work.
2. I am usually ready to listen and to begin work.
1. I need to be told to settle down, to listen, and to begin work.
0. I am never ready to listen and get to work.

PRESENTATIONS USING TECHNOLOGY

One of the most common presentation tools is PowerPoint. A high school teacher uses a rubric to assess both the technological expertise and the presentation skills of his students. PowerPoint areas on the rubric are:

- Number of slides
- Transitions
- Animation
- Creativity in bullet use
- Ease of reading
- Extras (chart, table, word art, slide master)
- Mechanics (spelling/grammar/typos). (R. Rakvic, computer teacher, Norwin High School, North Huntingdon, Pennsylvania, personal communication, May 18, 2011) His presentation areas include volume, eye contact, posture, clarity, introduction, and conclusion.

ONLINE CLASSES AND COMPONENTS

Once reserved for post-secondary courses, students in all grade levels are now taking online courses. According to one estimate, there are more than one million students in grades K–12 taking online courses (Gabriel, 2011). More and more high schools are *requiring* students to take a specific number of online courses before graduation. Although reduced per pupil cost is a benefit of online education, educators also feel obligated to prepare students for future online courses in college (Gabriel, 2011).

Moreover, as high school students become comfortable with online classes, more and more pressure is being put on instructors in higher education to provide online courses or online components for their classes. Chat rooms, threaded discussions or forums, wikis , and web logs or "blogs" are four areas of online assessments that require unique rubrics.

CHAT ROOMS

Some universities have contained online systems that provide professors with the ability to organize an in-house online chat room at a specific time with specific students in the course. This "closed" chat room feature is equipped with the ability of the professor to choose to be a part of the chat or to simply monitor students' comments on a specific topic. Although it is a virtual conversation, chat rooms can help to simulate a face-to-face classroom discussion. However, unlike the classroom discussions that are usually not recorded, complete transcripts of chat room comments are often available for grading.

Chat room rubrics to assess student participation usually include two areas: *skill* and *content*. Under *chat room skill,* the areas for consideration may include

- Promptness of logging on,

- Ability to respond to questions quickly,
- Capacity to maintain connection with the group,
- Comfort with the process as evidenced by the number of responses (Anderson, Bauer, and Speck, 2002).

Students who are slower typists or who are not comfortable with the chat room format may be unfairly penalized by slow or minimal responses.

Because computer comfort levels and skills can differ widely, evaluating chat room content separately is a must. Assessing the content of the chat room discussion parallels the evaluation of face-to-face discussions or class participation. A rubric that would assess the *content of a chat room* discussion may include these points:

- Comments contribute to the topic.
- Comments indicate the ability to follow the thread of the conversation.
- Responses are focused on the topic.
- The ability to answer questions that are posed is demonstrated.
- The ability to pose significant questions is demonstrated.
- The ability to make connections to course readings is demonstrated.
- Responses are clear and coherent. (Anderson, Bauer, and Speck, 2002)

An example of the complications caused by graded chat room conversations occurred when a student whose Internet connection was experiencing a difficulty became frustrated as she was continually being disconnected from the hour-long chat. Her professor, understanding her dismay, continued to tease her with, "Where's Amy?" or "Amy broke the Internet." For students who are concerned about grades, there may be little humor in those comments. Setting up chat room practice sessions prior to the graded session may benefit all students, especially those who are novices to the chat room format.

THREADED DISCUSSIONS OR FORUMS

Threaded discussions or forums, along with web logs (blogs) and wikis, differ from chat rooms in that these can be completed within a timeframe convenient to the student. The convenience of an asynchronous format (where there is no required time to log on) is appealing to many teachers and students.

In threaded discussions, questions or comments are posted for students' written responses. Students have access to their colleagues' comments and are invited to comment on those and to continue the thread of the discussion.

Rubrics for forum/threaded discussions include the same criteria that instructors use for evaluating essays with the addition of having students respond to colleagues' comments. A sample analytic rubric to assess on line forum responses is illustrated in box 9.1

BOX 9.1 Rubrics for Online Forum Discussions

QUALITY OF THE RESPONSE.

4. Addresses all aspects of the discussion question in depth. Able to make connections from content to other readings or to life experiences. ***Additional research evident and cited in APA format.***
3. Addresses all aspects of the question in depth. Able to make connections from content to other readings or to life experiences.
2. Answers all parts, but lacks depth or understanding. Minimal response.
1. Omits part(s) of question. Weak—lacks quality.

THOROUGHNESS OF RESPONSE TO CLASSMATES.

4. Appears to have read **at least four or more** previous discussions by due date and considered others' points of view before providing constructive criticism or support to others. May add another reply after original submission in response to others.
3. Appears to have read **at least three** previous discussions by due date and considered others' points of view before providing constructive criticism to others.
2. Appears to have read **at least two** previous discussions by due date and considered others' points of view before providing constructive criticism to others.
1. Appears to have read **only one** previous discussion by due date OR constructive criticism is unfounded.

APA FORMAT and FORMAL WRITTEN ENGLISH (MECHANICS, USAGE, SPELLING).

4. No errors
3. One or two errors
2. Three to five errors
1. More than five errors

DEADLINES

4. Submitted by due date and time
3. Posted within 24 hours of due date.
2. Posted 24–48 hours of due date
1. Over 48 hours late.

More than two days late will earn a zero for this section.

The brevity of a comparable holistic rubric used to evaluate on-line forums may be a time-saver for busy instructors. Note that this rubric does not evaluate grammatical errors or require citations.

HOLISTIC RUBRIC FOR ON LINE FORUM DISCUSSIONS

A score of 4 will be awarded for work that is beyond expectations.

3. Response shows use of all applicable sources and careful consideration of all parts of the question. Leaves constructive comments on another student's post.
2. Responds to all parts of the question with some discussion or some analysis of the material, drawing into the discussion literature from the class.
1. Response is partial, bland, or opinionated and lacks support of evidence or any analysis. OR submission is late.
0. Nothing submitted

BLOGS

A blog is an "online journal expressing the thoughts and interests of its author. Blogs are often updated frequently with personal thoughts, pictures and news related to the author's interests" (Blogging, 2003, para.1). Similar to social networking, these chronological electronic journals can be the forum for serious debates or light-hearted comments on a variety of topics. Because blogs and social networks are firsthand accounts, sometimes with unique points of view, they are very popular among a variety of people including teachers and students (Owyang, 2008).

Academic blogging has become very trendy among teachers of English, political science, and technology. As a required component of courses that are both face-to-face and online, blogging is a more personal form of threaded discussion and forces students to post writings for a wider audience than the threaded discussion or forum.

An analytic rubric for blogging often includes:

• reflections and connections to class work and readings,
• information/content/originality,
• presentation (errors in spelling, mechanics and formatting),
• multimedia enhancements(video, audio, images, etc.),
• community (links, comments on other blogs, or citing others including current research),
• number of postings. (Fisher, 2010; Poore, n.d.)

A description of the detailed holistic rubric used to evaluate university students' blogging is provided in box 9.2 The instructor uses the blog content as a "writing portfolio" for each student and explained, "I give students a broad range of topics on which to blog. I require them to blog the notes they use for their oral reports, and I occasionally devote class time to blogging. Rather than give them word count or frequency targets, I ask students to submit a blogging portfolio." The entire blog can be found at blogs.setonhill.edu/el267/2011/02/portfolio-1/.

Box 9.2 Holistic Blogging Rubric

5: Excellent:

  o By the due date, a working link points from this page to your portfolio.
  o Portfolio begins with a statement that not only informs a random visitor about the purpose of the course and the assignment, but also presents your ideas in an appealing, engaging way.
  o Each category is clearly marked, and introduced with a brief explanation of what the category label means.
  o Links point to two or more posts in each of these categories: Depth, Interaction, Discussion, and Timeliness.
  o Coverage category is thoughtfully presented.
  o In each category, posts are introduced with well-written, engaging explanations that show an awareness of how the informal writing is helping you learn.

4: Very Good:

  o By the due date, a working link points from this page to your blog, where it is possible to find the portfolio post.

---

o Portfolio begins with a statement that explains the purpose of the blog, in a manner that invites the interest of a random visitor.
o Each category section is clearly marked.
o Links point to an average of two posts in categories Depth, Interaction, Discussion, and Timeliness.
  ▪ The same post can appear in up to two different categories.
  ▪ The Coverage category is not the largest category.
o Posts are introduced with clear explanations of why the post belongs in the given category.

3: Acceptable:

o The link may be missing or malformed, but your portfolio is available on your blog.
o The portfolio statement informs the random visitor, but may be dry or perfunctory.
o Category divisions are all present, but they may not be clearly marked or defined.
o Links point to at least one unique post in Depth, Interaction, Discussion, and Timeliness; at least two of these categories feature more than one post; the same post does not appear in any more than two of these categories. The Coverage category demonstrates your efforts to learn from every blogging assignment.
o Posts may not all be introduced with clear explanations; introductions and links may be vague ("Here's my entry for this category" or "Click here to check out what I wrote.")

2: Good-faith Effort

o The portfolio entry is available on your blog.
o Some attempt at introducing the portfolio to an outside reader has been made.
o Some attempt at organizing the portfolio according to the categories (Depth, Interaction, Discussion, and Timeliness) has been made.
o At least one post has been assigned to each category, and some attempt to link to each post is evident.
o Some attempt has been made to introduce each post.

1: Partial

o Some evidence of an attempt to respond to at least part of the assignment.

0: No Submission

(Adapted with permission; D. Jerz , personal communication, April 30, 2011)

WIKIS

A wiki is a "database of pages which visitors can edit live" (Wiki.com, 2008, para. 1). Wiki participants collaborate in creating interactive web pages. Because wikis provide an easy way to exchange ideas and data on projects, reluctant students, who would not normally speak out, are encouraged to contribute. Moreover, since everyone is literally on the same page, there is no need for endless "reply-to-all" emails.

A professor from New York who uses wikis in her on-line course notes, "For each topic, I have article and/or text readings and then begin with a statement to help focus posts." The areas of evaluation on her rubric include:

- entry completed,
- collegial format,
- quality,
- timely. (Source: E. Lawerence, SUNY at Oneonta.)

Another analytic rubric for a wiki assignment may have the following assessment areas:

- Organization including headings and bulleted lists,
- Hyperlinks to credible sources,
- Attractiveness/graphics,
- Accuracy of information and citations,
- Mechanics (spelling, grammar, etc.),
- Creative use of Web 2.0 technology,
- Contributions to the group—participation. (NCTE, 2006)

PRODUCTS

The term "information literacy" applies to the ability to discern quality information from the sea of information on the Internet. With the click of a mouse or the tap of a finger, students are connected to a plethora of online activities and knowledge. Educational software, websites, and applications (apps) are three areas that require cautious evaluation.

EVALUATING EDUCATIONAL COMMERCIAL SOFTWARE

Teachers are often required to evaluate and determine the usability of computer software based on samples of the product. Although the quickest evaluations for software are simply checklists that indicate whether a component is present, an analytic rubric can help to provide a score to compare products. Educational value, format, ease of use, amount of interaction, and entertainment value are five areas often used to evaluate educational software. For some teachers, the determining factor has been whether the sound can be turned off easily. As one teacher indicated, "With 25 students using the same software, the noise level can be an issue."

The rubric below was created by a group of computer savvy college students who are studying to become elementary teachers. After examining educational software for math and reading, the group created the rubric and evaluated the software. They were especially proud of the descriptor, "Makes you want to throw it away" since we have all been at that frustration level.

The evaluation area of motivation was included after some of the software was "kid-tested." The pre-service teachers asked children to help evaluate the software and decided that the children's cheers and complaints would be a concrete way to assess its appeal. As one teacher explained, "If the kids don't like it, it doesn't matter how much we try to push it."

Rubric to Evaluate Educational Software

Key

4 = exceeds requirements
3 = meets requirements
2 = somewhat addresses requirements
1 = poorly addresses requirements
0 = requirement not met

- *Educational Value*

4. Beyond expectations for standards and learning goals.
   Meets a variety of goals and abilities.
   Higher order thinking skills obvious.
3. Meets standards; age appropriate.
2. Some educational value; does not address all required learning standards or goals.
1. Little educational value; may be entertaining only.
0. No educational value.

- *Ease of use*

    4. Very little if any coaching required; self-explanatory.
          Extremely easy to install and navigate.
          Quick response time.
    3. Easy to use with little teacher help; no frustration evident.
    2. Some difficulty at first, but will get easier with practice.
    1. Difficult and frustrating for most students at all times.
    0. Makes you want to throw it away!

- *Appearance*

    4. Extremely attractive, uncluttered, no apparent distractions.
          Background and font make it very easy to read.
    3. Visuals are attractive and focusing on items is easy.
          Text color and font make it easy to read.
    2. Bland; no visual punch. Font may be difficult to read.
    1. Cluttered; not sure where to look or where to click.
    0. Disappointing (Bland and difficult to read).

- *Clarity of purpose or ease of understanding*

    4. Challenging but not frustrating. Takes students beyond expectations.
          Logical order is evident.
          Students able to construct own knowledge from responses.
    3. Challenging and interesting.
          Engages the learner and takes students to higher level.
    2. Purpose is obvious; ease of use contributes to purpose.
    1. Difficult to understand purpose or meaning.
    0. Makes you ask, "What's the point?"

- *Student enthusiasm*

    4. Students cheer and beg to use. Excited and proud to learn the concept presented.
    3. Students are excited to use the software and learn new concepts. No complaints.
    2. Students are comfortable with the software. Few complaints.
    1. Most students complain about using.
    0. Students beg for anything but this one! (May be moaning!)

Source: Pre-service teachers, (2003). Seton Hill University, Greensburg, Pennsylvania.

EDUCATIONAL WEBSITES

With the staggering number of educational sites available, teachers have found that having two or three reliable sites for teacher resources as well as for student use can be a crucial time-saving factor. With that in mind, the evaluation of websites by teachers and by students can help illustrate that not all sites are created equal. The rubric in box 9.3 is used as an assignment for a class where students research math websites appropriate for student and/or teacher use. (An analysis paper and discussions are assigned to follow the rubric scoring.)

Box 9.3 Rubric for Teacher Evaluation of Websites

URL: http:// _____

Scoring Key:

4 = exemplary; 3 = good, basic, solid; 2 = weak; 1 = needs lots of work; 0 = not present.

Appearance and Navigation

- The website is labeled with text and images that give the site a clear identity.
- Pages load within a reasonable timeframe.
- The icons, menus, and directional symbols foster independent movement through the site by the user.
- The in-links allow you to quickly find your way to information on your topic of study.
- The page is labeled with the author's name and e-mail address.
- The graphics and art are functional and not merely decorative.
- The site is noncommercial or minimally commercial.

Content

- The spelling and grammar are correct.
- The information is current, accurate, and frequently updated.
- The subject matter is appropriate for the intended audience.
- The information is objective and free of biased viewpoints and images (such as gender, race).
- The information is sufficient in scope to adequately cover the topic for the intended audience.

- The out-links (links that take you to additional sites) are relevant and appropriate to the topic.
- Sound, video, and graphics are a good source of information and not merely entertainment.
- When used with a class, the information presented at this site stimulates imagination and curiosity.
- Using this site with a class promotes global awareness and appreciation of other cultures.
- Use of this site helps teachers develop online projects, collaborate with peers, and share information.
- I would use this site and recommend it to other teachers.

Total Points _____

Source: Adapted from Blue Web'n, 2005; Kalkman, 2003; Lerman, 2004; Payton, 2005

Helping students to become critical consumers of Internet information can start as early as the primary grades where students can be trained to look for dates and persons responsible for the site. Teachers are encouraged to discuss Internet credibility with students and help them to validate information. A simple research-filtering method is used by a middle school teacher who tells his students to avoid commercial sites by limiting their search to sites that end in .gov, .edu, or .org as opposed to .com.

A compilation of quality educational websites is available in *Essential Websites for Educational Leaders in the 21st Century* (Lerman, 2004). In this book, the author's criteria for the essential sites are

- Ease of access
- Content of value
- Ease of navigation
- Credibility/reliability of content
- Relevance for the reader
- Free-of-charge (Lerman, 2004, p. x).

APPLICATIONS (APPS)

The free-of-charge criterion was number one on a recent college-student-created rubric for mobile device applications. Although the rubric for Internet sites can be easily adapted to apps, a rubric developed exclusively for apps is illustrated in Box 9.4. The rubric creator added, "I had considered cost when crafting the rubric, but dropped it as I did not want it to carry the same weight as the other categories that I considered to be more important."

Box 9.4 Analytic Rubric for iPod and iPad Apps

Curriculum Connection

4. Skill(s) reinforced are strongly connected to the targeted skill or concept
3. Skill(s) reinforced are related to the targeted skill or concept
2. Skill(s) reinforced are prerequisite or foundation skills for the targeted skill or concept
1. Skill(s) reinforced in the app are not clearly connected to the targeted skill or concept

Authenticity

4. Targeted skills are practiced in an authentic format/problem-based learning environment
3. Some aspects of the app are presented in an authentic learning environment
2. Skills are practiced in a contrived game/simulation format
1. Skills are practiced in a rote or isolated fashion (e.g., flashcards)

Feedback

4. Feedback is specific and results in improved student performance; data are available electronically to student and teacher
3. Feedback is specific and results in improved student performance (may include tutorial aids)
2. Feedback is limited to correctness of student responses and may allow for students to try again
1. Feedback is limited to correctness of student responses

Differentiation

4. App offers complete flexibility to alter settings to meet student needs
3. App offers more than one degree of flexibility to adjust settings to meet student needs

---

2. App offers limited flexibility (e.g., few levels such as easy, medium, hard)
1. App offers no flexibility (settings cannot be altered)

User Friendliness

4. Students can launch and navigate within the app independently
3. Students need to have the teacher review how to use the app
2. Students need to have the teacher review how to use the app on more than one occasion
1. Students need constant teacher supervision in order to use the app

Student Motivation

4. Students are highly motivated to use the app and select it as their first choice from a selection of related choices of apps
3. Students will use the app as directed by the teacher
2. Students view the app as "more schoolwork" and may be off-task when directed by the teacher to use the app
1. Students avoid the use of the app or complain when the app is assigned by the teacher.

Adapted with permission from Walker, H. (2010). For permission to use, contact hwalker@bcps.org

SUMMARY

Schools in the United States have been scrambling to keep pace with the rapid growth in computer technology. The numbers of computers in both schools and at home have multiplied since the early 1990s and have been accompanied by a need for academic technological standards. State departments of education and national organizations have responded by setting technology benchmarks for schools, administrators, teachers, and students from kindergarten through college.

This chapter provided examples of assessing student work in the computer lab and in on-line classes. Rubrics for grading assignments of wikis, forums, and blogs were provided. Guidelines and rubrics to evaluate educational software, Internet websites, and applications were presented.

REFERENCES

Fisher, C. (2010). Blogging rubric. Retrieved April 30, 2011 from www.evenfromhere
.org/?p=1282.

Gabrielle, T. (2011, April 6). More pupils are learning online, fueling debate on quality. *New York Times,* p.A-1.

ISTE-NETS-S. (2011). Nets for students 2007. Retrieved April 21, 2011 from www
.iste.org/standards/nets-for-students/nets-for-students-2007-profiles.aspx.

ISTE-NETS-T. (2011). Nets for teachers 2008. Retrieved April 21, 2011 from www
.iste.org/standards/nets-for-teachers/nets-for-teachers-2008.aspx.

NCTE (2006). Wiki rubric. Read-write-think. Retrieved April 30, 2011 from www
.readwritethink.org/files/resources/lesson_images/lesson979/WikiRubric.pdf.

Nielson. (2009). Home Internet access in the US: Still room for growth. Retrieved
April 22, 2001 from www.marketingcharts.com/interactive/home-internet-access-
in-us-still-room-for-growth-8280/nielsen-internet-access-household-income-
february-2009jpg/.

Owyang, J. (2008). Understanding the difference between forums, blogs, and social
networks. *Web Strategy.* Retrieved April 30, 2011 from http://www.web-strategist.
com/blog/2008/01/28/understanding-the-difference-between-forums-blogs-and-
social-networks/.

Pew Internet and American Life Project. (2005). *Latest trends.* Who's online?
Internet adoption. Retrieved May 30, 2005: www.pewinternet.org/trends.
asp#demographics.

Poore. M. (n.d.). Assessing student blogs. Retrieved April 30, 2011 from blogagogy
.wordpress.com/assessing-blogs/.

Prensky, M. (2001). Digital natives, digital immigrants. *On the Horizon,* 9 (5), 1–6.
Retrieved June 10, 2011 from www.marcprensky.com/writing/Prensky%20-%20
Digital%20Natives,%20Digital%20Immigrants%20-%20Part1.pdf.

Walker, H. (2010). Evaluation rubric for iPod apps. Retrieved April 30, 2011 from
learninginhand.com/storage/blog/AppRubric.pdf.

Wiki (2008). What is a wiki? Retrieved April 30, 2011 from www.wiki.com.

Chapter 10

How to Create Your Own Rubrics

Live each day as you would climb a mountain. An occasional glance towards the summit puts the goal in mind. Many beautiful scenes can be observed from each new vantage point. Climb steadily, slowly, enjoy each passing moment; and the view from the summit will serve as a fitting climax to the journey.

—Joe Porcino

Nature-lover Joe Porcino's advice on life can be adapted for those teachers who decide to create their own scoring rubrics. That is, keep checking your objectives, review each step along the way, and try to enjoy the process.

In addition to that basic advice, there are specific steps and methods for creating your own rubrics. This chapter describes those steps and provides a recipe for creating your own rubric for any subject. Checklists for evaluating rubrics and some common scoring pitfalls are discussed. Samples of both clear and unclear rubrics are provided.

CREATING A RUBRIC

Teachers who have created their own rubrics describe a variety of methods. Some sort previously obtained samples of student product into three groups of high, medium, and low and begin to create descriptors from those samples. Others form a mental picture of the product and then jot notes of what the benchmark of quality should be. Many find an existing rubric and adapt it to their own specifications. All agree that flexibility is the key and to expect perfection can only result in frustration.

Box 10.1 contains a list of the suggested steps for creating your own rubrics and should be followed with a sense generosity to yourself. These are simply guidelines. As the teacher, you know your students best. Trust your instincts.

Box 10.1 Steps for Creating a Rubric

1. Focus on clear outcomes.
2. List three or four critical attributes of the performance/project.
3. Begin with the benchmark—the standard.
4. Develop statements that describe or define those qualities of performance short of expectations and beyond expectations.
5. Decide if the rubric will be analytic or holistic.
6. Research other rubrics.
7. Evaluate—Present the rubric to colleagues and students for input.
8. Do a practice test or a dry run if possible.
9. Revise as needed.
10. Share information. (Quinlan, 2009)

STEPS FOR CREATING RUBRICS

1. Focus on Clear Outcomes

The first step is somewhat understandable. Focusing on clear outcomes means keeping your eye on the goal. If you are considering using a rubric to assess student work, you probably have a specific project or assignment in mind. It is obviously more than a pencil and paper test and will require some subjective scoring decisions.

As you think of the project, ask yourself, "What are the reasons or the learning objectives for doing this? What do I want each child to learn?" Even if your goal is for students to have fun, there should still be some knowledge or skill attainment involved, or scoring accountability would not be needed.

You may be required to connect the project to national common core standards, state standards, school district goals, or even a local school goal. For example, perhaps students are required to create a commercial as a way of responding to a piece of literature. Although each state lists its own standards—with its own terminology—this activity meets one state goal of reading, analyzing, and interpreting literature.

In this list of academic standards, students by third grade should be able to "identify literary elements in stories describing characters, setting, and plot."

By grade 11, students are expected to "analyze the relationships, uses, and effectiveness of literary elements used by one or more authors in similar genres including characterization, setting, plot, theme, point of view, tone, and style" (Pennsylvania Department of Education, n.d.a., p. 6).

This activity also ties into a national literacy goal. The National Council of Teachers of English and the International Reading Association have listed as part of their Literacy Goal 3, "Students apply a wide range of strategies to comprehend, interpret, evaluate, and appreciate texts" (Read Write Think, n.d.). Although the same activity could meet a district goal of reading to increase assessment scores or a school goal of responding to literature in creative ways or even providing entertainment for a PTA meeting, teachers usually focus the rubric to assess whatever it is they want the students to learn.

2. List Three or Four Critical Attributes of the Performance or Project

As you think of the project, decide what is critical for you as the teacher and for the objectives you have identified. Are grammar and spelling important enough to subtract points? With a group of pre-service teachers in a college setting, the answer would be "yes." With a group of emergent literacy first-graders, the answer may be "not at all." Is neatness important? Are there a minimum or maximum number of pages required? All areas need to be considered, *but not all need to be included on the rubric.*

Consider the project discussed above to create a literature commercial. If the teachers were aiming for the standards of understanding of literary elements of character, setting, and plot, then those elements would be a required component and would need to be listed on the rubric. A major caution is that teachers often want to evaluate many more than three or four critical areas. The advice to newcomers is to be kind to yourself and do not try to evaluate every dimension. However, you may want to list them all in your rough draft, for this will help when you get to the decision needed in step 5.

3. Describe the Expected Qualities— or what does a Good one Look Like?

Those who write about rubrics generally agree that teachers should limit their use of rubrics to projects with which they are familiar. The notebook rubrics that were discussed in chapter 5 (see boxes 5.3 and 5.4) are good examples of rubrics created by teachers who were familiar with the types of notebooks their students traditionally submitted.

To describe the expected qualities of the assessment, it is helpful to have samples of relevant student work. For the experienced teacher, it may be enough to recall previous student work without having the actual samples. For the novice teacher, an experienced colleague may be an excellent source of information on what to expect or "what a good one looks like."

One of the simplest explanations of the 4-point scoring rubric is the flower drawing. In this model, the teacher introduces a 4-point scoring rubric by using something familiar to all students—drawing a flower scene. She begins by dividing a poster board into four parts. In the first part she draws only a circle and labels it with the numeral 1.

She asks her class if the drawing of a flower is complete. When they respond "no," she moves to the second square, draws another circle, adds a line to represent a stem, and labels it with a 2. The students are again aware that more is needed for it to be a flower.

In the third square, the teacher adds leaves and petals to make a daisy-like flower. Many children now declare that the picture is complete, but she cautions them to wait until they have seen her "best effort." She then completes square numbered 4 with background filling in all the white area with many colors (Harmon, 2001).

To clarify a score of zero, some teachers include an empty square in the presentation. Because it simplifies and clarifies the 4-point category of "beyond expectations," the flower model is appropriate for all ages. Audience response to this simple example is usually very positive. As one college student exclaimed, "I never really understood rubrics until I saw the flower example."

The expected quality is often the standard or benchmark. In a 4-point rubric, this would be the paper that would earn a score of *three*. It is critical to remember that no matter what we have come to believe about numerical grade-point averages, on a 4-point scoring rubric, it is the *three* that is connected to the A while the 4 is reserved for that student who would earn the A plus. (See chapter 12 for converting rubric scores into grades.)

4. Develop Clear and Precise Statements that Describe Performance Short of Expectations and Beyond Expectations

Articulating specific and measurable descriptions for performance attributes can get tricky. If prior student samples are available, it is sometimes helpful to sort them into three categories of excellent, poor, and those in between.

A life science teacher had students create scientific diagrams of various organisms. During the scoring process, his first sweep would be to sort them into three piles. As he was quickly going through them, if any drawings amazed him as illustrations that went beyond the requirements, he would place those in a fourth pile.

He explained, "Those piles became the basis for the revised rubrics I cre-ated for the next time. Once students saw the quality of the drawings that earned the highest score of 4, the quality of all work improved—including attention to correct spelling of the labels."

Watch for vague terminology in rubric descriptors. An example of vague descriptors was evident in an analytic rubric created for a scientific report at the high school level. Under grammar and spelling, the point values and the descriptors were

1 point—Very frequent grammar and spelling errors.
2 points—More than two errors.
3 points—Only one or two errors.
4 points—All spelling and grammar are correct.

The weak part of the above rubric is between the scores of one and two. At what number does "more than two errors" become "very frequent"? Is it five or greater? This teacher probably knew what "very frequent" looked like and needed to communicate that to the students. If teachers can quantify descriptors such as "very frequent," they will simplify and clarify the assessment procedure.

An excerpt of another rubric using vague descriptors is a 4-point rubric required to be used by college supervisors for final evaluation of student teachers. The descriptor for excellence is "The candidate *consistently* and *thoroughly* demonstrates indicators of performance"; superior states, "The candidate *usually* and *extensively* demonstrates indicators of performance." The other two scoring areas use the terms *sometimes* and *adequately*, while the lowest score is described with *rarely* or *never* and *inappropriately or superficially* (Pennsylvania Department of Education, n.d.b., p. 5).

Using terms such as *thoroughly* for one score and *extensively* for a lower score calls for a subjective judgment on the part of the observers. In all instances, being able to quantify the descriptors can help to avoid confusion and conflict and guarantee consistency among a variety of scorers known as *inter-rater reliability*.

A well-know textbook author suggests using the descriptor "rarely or never" for a score of one point on a 4-point rubric. The question remains, if students *never* exhibit the trait, how do they earn a point? ALWAYS include a "zero" on rubrics for work not submitted.

5. Decide Holistic or Analytic

At some point in your rubric creating, you must decide if you want to evaluate the entire project as a whole or if you want to dissect the assignment into its specific components. Because the complexity or simplicity of the task will determine the number of traits to include for assessment, this is the time to double-check the list of attributes that you created in step 2.

As the name implies, a holistic rubric evaluates the entire project and yields one numerical score (usually between 0 and 4 or 0 and 6). A holistic rubric is used when teachers want to evaluate the entire product or performance based on their overall impression of the work. The critical components are listed as the benchmark items under item 3 in a 4-point rubric, or under item 5 in a 6-point rubric.

For example, if using a holistic rubric to evaluate a student's assignment to deliver an oral commercial for a piece of literature, the benchmark or critical components may be that the commercial includes all the required components or elements of fiction as listed, the student's presentation is audible, and the audience was interested. The exemplary top score would be for the very creative commercial.

In comparison, the analytic rubric actually dissects the project and provides a separate score for each item or component. A total score is obtained by the addition of all the points earned. There is no set requirement for the number of traits to incorporate in an analytic rubric. It may be as few as 2 or as many as 10 or more.

Once again, the evaluator should feel free to include all traits deemed necessary for evaluation. In the example of the commercial, one area might be for including all literary elements, another area may be the components of an oral presentation, a third may be for holding the audience's interest, and another for creativity.

Although some experts feel that holistic rubrics are quicker and easier to use, the analytic rubric can actually save scoring time because all possible conditions and scenarios are addressed since each attribute earns its own score. The notebook rubrics in figures 5.3 and 5.4 illustrate the differences between holistic and analytic rubrics. Again, the teacher's objectives should be reflected in the choice of rubric. (See chapter 2 for additional information on analytic and holistic rubrics.)

6. Research Existing Rubrics

"Using rubrics is easy; creating rubrics is hard!" This quote from a novice teacher sums up the rubric philosophy for many. However, that difficulty in creating your own rubric can be simplified with the aid of your colleagues and the Internet. Once you decide what your objective is—what you want to assess—you can begin your search for existing rubrics to meet your needs.

There is a wealth of sample rubrics available online for teacher use. Type the words "scoring rubric" into any search engine, and a number of rubric sites will be available. Several sites even provide the capability to personalize rubrics with your own name and school name. (Some of the best teacher-tested rubric sites are listed in the appendix)

Scoring rubrics are also often available in teacher manuals and in commercially produced books. Many of these sample rubrics can serve as a basis for adaptations for the specific requirements of the teacher or can be used as they are. Using an existing rubric is often a good way for a novice to begin using rubrics. Existing rubrics provide both confidence and a foundation for future use.

Some questions to ask if using an existing rubric include:

- Does the rubric meet the objectives?
- Are there qualities that are missing, or are there items that are not a part of the assignment?
- Will the students and their parents understand the terminology? Is it developmentally appropriate?
- Are the descriptors well defined, or are they vague and subject to the scorer's interpretation?

Answering those questions can help teachers to clarify and refine existing rubrics.

Blanket statements of "A score of 4 will be earned when work is beyond expectations" and "A zero will be earned if work is missing or unable to be scored" can be listed at the top of the rubric. This shortcut will enable thorough descriptors for areas one though three.

7. Present the Rubric to Colleagues and Students for Input

Even if you are using a commercially prepared rubric, getting input from colleagues and students can help to refine the rubric and clarify the descriptors. Although you may know what you mean by "usually," you should reword that term into a numerical value. Students are typically comfortable in assigning reasonable numerical values to scoring guidelines.

As one middle school teacher realized, "They [the students] are a great resource." Student input also provides "ownership" for the rubric, which can be vital for cooperation, effort, and student achievement.

8. Do a Practice Run if Possible

There is a variety of ways to "test drive" any rubric. An old set of papers can provide a practice test of the rubric. You can use that sample set to score yourself or even have students or other teachers practice scoring a sample set of papers using the rubric.

If a practice run is not feasible, an alternative is simply to jump in using the rubric with an "assurance policy." The assurance policy means that you assure your students that if they are unhappy with their scores, you are willing to rescore without the rubric based on your opinion of the work.

Another strategy is to use the "pre-scoring agreement." This is a disclaimer that you, the teacher, always reserve the right to grade on your prior knowledge of the assignment and not use the rubric. However, once teachers and students get comfortable with using rubrics, these backup strategies are seldom needed.

9. Revise as Needed

Rubrics are works in progress. Teachers who use rubrics realize that no matter how experienced they are, or how many projects they have graded, there is always the possibility of a surprise. For example, if you have not included using double space as a requirement for a paper, it is really not fair to subtract points for the student who single-spaced. However, you may want to make a note of it so that double spacing will be included on the next rubric.

Remember the special education teacher who revealed that she actually jots notes on the back of students' work as a reminder of skills that must be addressed the next time. In a similar example, you should agree with the scores. If adhering to the rubric results in a student's product being scored lower (or higher) than you believe it deserves, the rubric needs to be revised.

An example of the revision process of a rubric/expanded checklist is illustrated below. Professors of a teacher education program wanted some way to assess the affective aspect of their students in methods classes. As a group, they created an expanded checklist.

After using the rubric for several semesters, the instructors met to discuss revision. One newcomer to the program needed clarification on the pass/fail of the original document. She was confused about what was meant by failure and was concerned that failing the rubric meant failing the course. Others discussed what they used as a description for each item, and it was decided to include these.

The revised rubric is in box 10.2. The parts in italics are the new additions.

Three revisions of the tool were created before all agreed on the form as shown in box 10.2. The revised tool clarifies what it means to fail the rubric and added descriptors to each item. Although it is not a numerical score rubric, it does meet the definition of a tool used to evaluate. At the end of the year, the instructors meet to share experiences, student comments, and recommendations for future revisions.

Box 10.2 *Revised* **Education Program Professional Rubric**

NAME _____ INSTRUCTOR _____

COURSE _____ TERM _____

RUBRIC GRADE (Pass/Fail) _____

S—satisfactory performance

N—need for improvement (deficiency)

Three deficiencies constitute student *failure of the rubric.*

_____ Student practices professional behavior. (*Student demonstrates positive expectation of self and class; is enthusiastic about own learning; demonstrates appropriate behavior in classroom; accepts constructive criticism and modifies behavior accordingly.*)

COMMENTS:

_____ Student is conscientious about attendance and punctuality. (*Student regularly attends class on time; submits work in a timely fashion; notifies instructor prior to absence.*)

COMMENTS:

_____ Student communicates effectively in written English. (*Student written work demonstrates ability to write thematically in a grammatically correct fashion.*)

COMMENTS:

_____ Student communicates effectively in spoken English. (*Student demonstrates in-class discussion and presentation skills that are cogent and grammatically correct.*)

COMMENTS:

_____ Student appropriately and respectfully participates in class discussions. (*Student is open to, and actively participates in, discussion and exchange of ideas and views.*)

COMMENTS:

_____ Student displays potential for assertiveness and strong classroom presence. (*Student is a contributing member of the class and an effective oral presenter.*)

COMMENTS:

If a student receives a failing grade on this rubric in two or more courses, the student and her/his education advisor will create a plan of corrective action. Lack of improvement in deficient areas may result in denial of student teaching privilege. A copy of this rubric is maintained in the student's file.

Reprinted with permission: D. Gray, Education Division, Seton Hill University, Greensburg, Pennsylvania (Personal communication, June 9, 2011.)

10. Share Information

Parents and students need to be informed of the rubric that you use for assessment purposes. The rubric is a concrete tool for communicating what you value in a particular assignment. Many schools post rubrics on their websites and make sure that parents receive hard copies at parents' night, during conferences, or with letters of explanation.

One warning must be considered before distributing the rubric. If the rubric is full of educational buzzwords, it should be revised for all to understand. Asking someone outside of the profession to read the rubric can help to clarify terms. A colleague, who writes for professional educational journals, asks her accountant husband to read her writing for clarity. "If Jim can't understand it, I know I have to rewrite."

EVALUATING THE EVALUATION

When evaluating a rubric, there are three major areas of consideration: *reliability*, *validity*, and *utility*. A reliable rubric will produce consistent scores from a variety of scorers or from just you over a period of time. A valid rubric will meet the objectives and reflect teaching content. Utility in a rubric refers clarity of terms and to the ease of scoring. Questions to ask when evaluating your rubric are similar to those questions that are asked when an existing rubric is being used.

- Does the rubric meet the objectives of the assignment?
- Does the rubric reflect what you emphasize in your teaching?
- Does the highest scale point represent a truly exemplary—beyond expectations—performance or product? Remember it is not necessary to have students score at every point level, but they need to know what a good one looks like.

- Are the descriptors clear? Are students able to understand what you mean?
- Would other scorers reach the same results as you (inter-rater reliability)?
- After using the rubric, do you agree with all the scores? (Arter and Mc-Tighe, 2001; Herman, Aschbacher, and Winters, 1992)

CAUTIONS WHEN SCORING

Culham and Spandell (1993) identify some pitfalls that those of us who use rubrics for scoring should try to avoid:

Leniency or harshness error—being too hard or too easy on everyone. Although this consistency is better than being extra generous or extra harsh with just a few students, teachers still need perspective. One way to avoid variations in perspective is to score all papers during the same time frame. We all have good and bad days, and by scoring with a rubric, teachers can often avoid those influences. As one converted rubric user admitted, "I think my grading [when using a rubric] is less subject to whims, moods, and biases."

Trait error—too hard or too easy on a given trait. Again, the consistency of the scorer is the crucial element. One college professor was obsessed with proper use of citation guidelines and was extremely strict when students did not adhere to the prescribed format. Because he was consistently harsh, students soon realized that proper citations were important enough to use with care.

Appearance—We are all pleased when students obviously take time to create neat or aesthetically pleasing products. Nevertheless, if neatness or artistic ability is not included on the rubric, it is not fair to consider that in grading. However, it is in those situations that the exemplary score of "beyond expectations" is earned.

Length—Beware of the temptation to increase a score based on length. Most teachers agree that longer is not necessarily better. One high school teacher told his advanced students that their research papers should not be more than eight typed double-spaced pages. He announced, "I will read eight pages. If your paper is more than eight pages, please indicate which eight pages you would like me to read."

Fatigue—Although some teachers prefer to grade in one sitting, frequent breaks may be needed to view work with fresh eyes. Teachers often plan to allot a specific time to grading papers. The science teacher who is assessing student drawings uses Saturday morning for evaluations. Using the rubric, he can assess 50 or so drawings before lunch. However, he admits that if this were 50 research papers, he would need more than one morning to fairly assess each one.

Comparison effect—If the last five papers have been awful, an average one may be granted a higher score by comparison. In the same framework, if the last five have been exemplary, an average may earn a lower score than it deserves. If this situation occurs, it may be a good indication that the rubric needs to be revised for future use.

Personality bias—Watch for your own opinions to color your point of view—both pro and con are at work here. Teachers who do not agree with the chosen position of a research paper may be likely to be more critical of that work than of a work with which they agree. Another example of the personality factor is when teachers recognize the name of a student who always does excellent work, they may actually grade "up" giving a higher score because of that bias.

Skimming—Short cuts are tempting when grading a stack of papers, but unless it is the initial sorting, quick skims are not advisable. Again, in fairness to each student, each work should be granted the same degree of attention.

Discomfort at making judgments—It is important to realize that you are grading a work, not a person. The messages you send about what you value must be consistent. (Remember the professor with the citation obsession.)

No matter how often we have used a reliable rubric, there are often gray areas or surprises in student work that fall between descriptors. Sometimes it helps to put the "gray area" project aside to see if other projects have the same attribute and then be consistent in grading those. These unique projects can also provide a basis for rubric revision. When in doubt, a good question to ask is, "If this were my child's project, how would I want this handled?"

SUMMARY

Teachers who are searching for a fair way to score subjectively-assessed products often rely on scoring rubrics to facilitate the scoring procedure. Teachers may adopt existing rubrics, may adapt existing rubrics to fit their needs, or may choose to create their own. In all scenarios, specific steps are recommended when teachers create rubrics, adapt rubrics, or evaluate existing rubrics.

The key points of creating rubrics include:

• Begin with a familiar activity or project.
• Research sample rubrics.

- Don't expect perfection.
- Begin with the standard or benchmark and then describe work beyond and below that standard.
- Don't try to assess everything in one assignment.
- Work with peers.
- Get student input. (Quinlan, 2003)

Even though using a rubric to assess student work can help to clarify expectations and eliminate bias, there are scoring cautions for teachers to consider. This chapter has provided guidelines for adapting or creating scoring rubrics to meet individual objectives. Evaluation of rubrics and common scoring pitfalls were also addressed.

REFERENCES

Arter, J., and McTighe, J. (2001). *Scoring rubrics in the classroom: Using performance criteria for assessing and improving student performance.* Thousand Oaks, CA: Corwin Press.

Culham, R., and Spandell, V. (1993). *Problems and pitfalls encountered by raters.* Portland, OR: Northwest Regional Educational Laboratory for the Oregon Department of Education.

Harman, N. (2001). Student implementation of the rubric. In G. L. Taggart, S. J. Phifer, J. A. Nixon, and M. Wood (Eds.), *Rubrics: A handbook for construction and use* (pp. 37–44). Lanham, MD: Scarecrow.

Herman, J., Aschbacher, P., and Winters, L. (1992). *A practical guide to alternative assessment.* Alexandria, VA: Association for Supervision and Curriculum Development.

Pennsylvania Department of Education. (n.d.a.). *Academic standards for reading, writing, speaking and listening.* Retrieved June 9, 2005: www.pde.state.pa.us/k12/lib/k12/RWSLStan.doc.

Pennsylvania Department of Education. (n.d.b.). *Testing requirements* (Links to student teacher assessment forms). Retrieved June 9, 2005: www.teaching.state.pa.us/teaching/cwp/view.asp?a=90andpm=1andQ=32539.

Quinlan, A. M. (2010, April). How to create scoring rubrics: Appropriate assessment for math today. Paper presented at National Council of Teachers of Mathematics, International Meeting, San Diego, CA.

Quinlan, A. M. (2003, November). Scoring rubrics: Appropriate assessment for adolescents. Paper presented at the National Middle School Association 30th Annual Conference and Exhibit, Atlanta, GA.

Read Write Think. (n.d.). IRA/NCTE standards for the English language arts. Retrieved June 9, 2005: www.readwritethink.org/standards/.

Chapter 11

Student-Generated Rubrics

Learning is not attained by chance; it must be sought for with ardor and attended to with diligence.

—Abigail Adams

When former first lady Abigail Adams made those comments concerning learning, she probably could not have envisioned the changes in the American education system today. However, we may imagine her pleasure if she knew that today successful teachers still plan for the achievement of their students with both ardor and diligence.

Teachers who are teaching for achievement and for excellence are often followers of learner-centered teaching. An important component of the learner-centered philosophy is having students actively involved in their own assessment. One way to accomplish this is with student-generated rubrics.

Using student-generated rubrics is a proven, practical strategy for involving learners in the assessment process. By creating a rubric with their teacher before completing the assignment, students increase their ownership in the process of evaluating their work. As they accept ownership of the process, the learners become more motivated to produce quality work. In addition, providing feedback is one of the "greatest sources of intrinsic motivation" educators can provide to their students (Jensen, 2005, p.110).

This chapter describes learner-centered teaching as it relates to assessment, discusses background on student-generated rubrics, and provides examples of how to guide students through the rubric-creating process. Self-assessment and peer-assessment issues are also addressed.

Chapter 11

LEARNER-CENTERED TEACHING

Learner-centered teaching (also referred to as student-centered learning) is a perspective of education that concentrates all educational decisions with the student as the primary focus (Jensen, 2005; McCombs and Whistler, 1997). That means that the student is at the center of learning.

Although this seems practical, the opposite of learner-centered is the teacher-centered philosophy of the 1960s. In those days, teachers were taught that the classroom was their stage and they (the teachers) were the stars. However, in the learner-centered paradigm, the teacher is often the "supporting actor"; it is the student who has star billing.

While learner-centered can be difficult to define, experienced administrators recognize it when they see it. An elementary teacher friend once worked for a principal who used a checklist to assess the learner-centered environment of each classroom. That checklist included the following description of a learner-centered classroom:

- Student-created projects and all student work on display (not just the best)
- Chairs around tables for interaction or desks in groupings
- Teacher desk *not* front and center
- Teacher *not* front and center (often working with students and difficult to locate)
- Multiple activities occurring simultaneously
- Students learning from each other (good learning noises)
- Student choice and voice evident in planning

Two items on that list were memorable to that teacher. They were that if you came to the door of the classroom, it would take you a moment or two to find the teacher, because she was in working with the students and not standing in front of the room. The other characteristic had to do with desk arrangements: The teacher desk should not be in the front, and the student desks should not be in straight rows of single desks. For teachers who like to be in control at all times, this can create a threatening feeling. However, teachers often change the student desk configuration depending on learning strategies for the day (Jensen, 2005).

Another description of a learner-centered environment has components describing the students that are reflected in the environmental checklist. In this description of the students in a learner-centered classroom, the students

- Are challenged
- Are given an explanation of what is expected

- Are given choice and control
- Are encouraged to work cooperatively
- Work with material that is personally interesting and relevant
- Believe they have the personal competence to succeed
- Feel that their opinions are valued and respected
- Have individualized attention to personal learning preferences
- Have some input into what standards and methods will be used for evaluation (Lemov, 2010; McCombs and Whistler, 1997)

STUDENT-GENERATED RUBRICS

A middle school teacher who reviewed the above list discovered that he actually meets all nine of the learner-centered characteristics when he employs student input into a scoring rubric. He said that he was not aware of attempting to employ learner-centered methods when he decides to get student input in the rubric. "When I ask students what they need to have included in a rubric, I am actually challenging them to reflect on the project and am giving them choices and some control."

He continued that he always includes some of his own nonnegotiable items in the rubric such as correct spelling. "The students respect that because they know that I respect their input. It's not enough to ask them, you actually have to use their ideas."

Teachers at all levels who subscribe to the learner-centered philosophy are quick to see the advantage of using student-generated rubrics or bringing students into the assessment process. Excellent teachers ". . . get students busily engaged in productive, positive work" (Lemov, 2010, p. 149).

Educators have long known that when students are brought into the assessment process, assessments become more meaningful (Anderson, 1998; Skillings and Ferrell, 2000). As one teacher described it, "They have great suggestions. Sometimes they think of things that would not be significant to me, but [are] vital to them."

For example, two groups of seventh grade biology students were grouped according to math ability—algebra and general math. The science students who were in the general math group referred to themselves as the "dumb ones." The teacher told them, "No, you are the students who *choose* to take general math!" Interestingly, when it came to student-generated rubrics for their science projects, this group always allotted more weight to creativity than their peers who were taking algebra.

Immediately, they were participating actively in the assignment and knew their own strengths! These "students who chose to take general math" were free to develop their strengths by their input on how they were graded even though it was clear that some criteria were declared "nonnegotiable."

One teacher added that having students help to create assessment tools contributes to a sense of community in his classroom and helps to reduce anxiety and stress. This was revealed when a second grader asked, "You mean to get the best grade, all I have to do is what is on that 'roof brick'?"

Sometimes referred to as "negotiable contracting," the practice of empowering students does not mean that teachers have given up their traditional roles (Jensen, 2005; Lemov, 2010; Stix, 1997). On the contrary, teachers who are confident in their role of authority are also comfortable in empowering their students to become valued partners in the assessment process. In reality, teachers and students must come to a mutually acceptable agreement (Skillings and Ferrell, 2000). As teachers lead and guide the negotiation process, they are providing students with a model for real-life compromise.

The significance of student input in the assessment process was evident in the comments of a college professor. She was not happy with the gray assessment area of classroom discussion in her own courses and had decided to ask for student suggestions. Admittedly reluctant to hand over any of her power, she confessed that her students proposed criteria that really tested her commitment to learner-centered instruction to the limit. They suggested that right and wrong answers in oral discussions would count equally. That made her very uncomfortable, and she expressed her concern to the class.

The students responded by making the point that once a student makes an error in a discussion, it is difficult to be courageous enough to try again. They also argued that teachers should support the belief that students learn from errors. With doubts, the instructor agreed that right and wrong answers counted equally in classroom discussions.

By the end of the semester, the instructor recognized the benefits of that simple change in assessment. Not only was there an increase in the quantity of responses, which was expected, but the quality of student contribution also increased. Even the typically shy students of all ages can become comfortable with giving opinions and sharing experiences (Lemov, 2010; Rhem, 1996).

Other proponents of gleaning input from students echo the delight in student improvement. A middle level teacher in South Carolina added that when she started having the children help to design the rubric prior to the project assignment, student achievement soared. She wrote, "Wow! What a difference this made in the end results. When I talked to the classes and asked what made them improve, most said that they understood what was expected."

She also made an interesting point that often various sections of the same course will view different items as being vital. As long as the integrity of the project was intact, the teacher was comfortable in assigning different values for the same item in different sections. Some classes wanted creativity to have more weight; other sections wanted neatness to be a vital component. Because of the mutual respect, the teacher and her students usually managed to find solutions without compromising the learning objective.

Relinquishing some of this control is not always easy for teachers who have been the authority figure for years. A curriculum resource teacher told a group of administrators, "I am constantly working with teachers making them feel comfortable sharing the rubric with the students and allowing the students to begin to 'own' the scoring details of their papers. It's not always easy."

One reason that teachers are reluctant to get students involved in the grading process is that developing rubrics with students can be time consuming. When class time has to be taken from content teaching, teachers who are accountable for student achievement on statewide assessment tests often feel as though they cannot spare the time.

However, as with any new learning, the major investment of time occurs at the beginning. As students become more comfortable with the process, the rubrics are created rather quickly. Teachers who have set aside time for student input are usually rewarded with improved student product. An educator from Tennessee who often gleans student input in rubrics writes, "I have also found that when the teaching focus is on helping students learn how to learn, and students participate in the development of rubrics, they are clearer about what is expected from them. As a result they learn more from the task" (Anderson, 1998, p.13).

HOW TO GET STUDENTS INVOLVED

Although some teachers may be reluctant to get student input, their students are seldom reluctant to contribute their ideas on how to be assessed. What may be difficult is getting students to understand what types of things to include. One successful method in developing a 4-point analytic rubric is described by Anderson (1998), which she calls "four-by-four" (p. 12). In this small group process,

- Each group is required to identify four characteristics of good quality in the task or project.
- These four characteristics from each group are listed for all to see on the board, overhead, or chart paper.
- "Reporters" from each group explain the four traits from their group and answer questions about the four traits.
- After each group has presented, the instructor and the entire class together decide on the four traits vital to the task.

- The students are then to return to their groups to write four descriptors for each of the four traits and the corresponding point value (usually 1 to 4).
- After another sharing with the class, a consensus is reached and the rubric is completed. (Anderson, 1998).

Another teacher uses a similar method starting with six traits. In this process students in groups are required to list six criteria for the given project. From that list of six, they are to rank their six from most to least important. The top two from each group are listed on the board and are discussed with the ultimate goal of listing no more than four traits. Students are then asked to describe a project that would be the benchmark (what a good one will look like) as well as work that would be beyond and work that would fall short of their criteria (Stix, 1997).

A shorter process is for the teacher to present an existing rubric for adaptations. In this process, students view an existing rubric (possibly obtained from the Internet) that describes the task, such as an oral presentation. After reviewing the rubric, students are asked to add or delete traits as appropriate.

A variation of this process is used when teachers present the rubrics they would like to use and simply get student input on the descriptors and weights of the scores. This can be done in groups as above or as a whole-class activity. As always, the teacher should determine ahead of time which traits are nonnegotiable. Surprisingly, some classes accept the rubric as presented and suggest no changes. Simply being consulted is enough to garner support for the rubric.

Other surprises can also develop. After years of working with middle school students who always asked, "Is this for a grade?" a college professor was working with her class of pre-service teachers on a rubric for an informal sharing of literacy strategies. To her surprise, students requested that they *not* be graded on the presentation.

Although the instructor was concerned as to the quality of presentations without the attached assessment score, she reluctantly agreed. Not only were the presentations excellent, many of the students mentioned this assignment in their final evaluations of the course. They discussed how refreshing and liberating it was to prepare for colleagues without the concern of a grade. One wrote, "Finally we're treated as adults," and another declared, "It made me feel like a real teacher!"

TEACHING STUDENTS ABOUT RUBRICS

Teachers who are getting student input on scoring rubrics make sure that students know what a rubric is. Once students understand the concept of scoring with rubrics, they actually create them quite quickly. Obviously, students who have had prior experiences with rubrics are usually comfortable with the format. The rubric for classroom behavior that was discussed in chapter 3 (see box 3.4) was created by second graders who were familiar with assessment by rubric.

A kindergarten teacher claims that her students are quite familiar with rubrics from the first day of school when they work to earn a smiley face. This teacher uses a stamp with either happy face or a straight-mouthed face when assessing work.

Visitors watching her glean the criteria for an illustrated sequence of *Goldilocks and the Three Bears* are quick to realize that these students know that to earn the happy face. They know that they must have three pictures that show beginning, middle, and end; the pictures must be in order; they must have used at least three different colors; and it must be their neatest work. Anything less than that will earn the straight face.

The teacher explained, "I never use a frowning face. For my students, a face with a frown could be devastating." Students were encouraged to remember the requirements as they worked and all seemed to qualify for the happy-face stamp.

Another elementary teacher uses students' answers to questions about their work to help explain the scoring. Similar to a rubric described by Andrade (1997), this rubric is sometimes called the "Yes, but" scoring method and uses examples from "YES, AND" all the way to "NO" to explain a four-point rubric:

- "Yes, (I did . . .) AND . . ." means they did more than was expected to earn 4 points.
- "Yes" means they met the basic requirements for 3 points.
- "Yes, (I did . . .) BUT (I did not) . . ." usually means they forgot something and have earned 2 points.
- "No, (I did not) . . . BUT (I did) . . ." indicates that although they did not do most of the assignment, they did include something, which would be a score of 1 point.
- A flat "No" indicates that they did not submit the assignment and earned the zero.

She explained that she has also used this same questioning technique for each component of an analytic rubric, and although this is an elementary process, many levels of students with varying abilities would benefit from the example.

One of the simplest explanations for the scoring criteria of a rubric for all grades is the four-point flower rubric as described in chapters three and ten.

SELF-ASSESSMENT AND PEER ASSESSMENT

Once students understand rubric formats, they can easily evaluate their own work. According to Rolheiser and Ross (n.d.), benefits associated with student self-evaluation include increased motivation and a more positive attitude toward assessment.

When discussing student self-assessment, a middle school teacher relates, "The best way that I have found is to provide them with a rubric prior to completing the assignment. Then, they turn that rubric in with a score that they have given themselves for each area. We either conference or they write me a letter justifying their scoring. I have found that students actually tend to be tougher on themselves than most teachers would be." She adds that she models the process before students are expected to work independently.

The letter-writing justification activity also works in a peer-assessment format. Ainsworth and Christinson (1998) suggest that when having peers assess each other, it is vital to have students work in pairs chosen by the teacher. Considerations for assigning peer assessment partners may be based on matching different levels of ability, behavior combinations, and special needs.

Peer partnerships should be maintained over a sufficient period of time so that students can establish a working relationship, but changed periodically to enable students to experience a variety of peer partners. Another caution in using peer assessment is to demonstrate that comments must be limited to the rubric. Children often want to simply say, "Good job" and be finished or score friends higher than deserved. Teachers who use peer assessment often model the process to illustrate how to make specific comments limited to and based upon the rubric.

SUMMARY

Having students' input in generating rubrics is a proven, practical activity that directly involves students in the assessment process. By creating a rubric with their teacher before completing the assignment, students gain ownership of the process of evaluating their work, and they become more motivated to produce quality work.

Using student-generated rubrics can help to support activities in a learner-centered environment. As students participate in creating scoring rubrics, they glean a deeper understanding of what needs to be accomplished to perform a task well. In addition, as students describe their expected criteria, they develop a sense of community and eliminate sources of stress and anxiety.

Teachers who include student input in rubric development are often pleasantly surprised at the outcome. They have learned that including students in the rubric-creating process at all levels helps students become more aware of and committed to their learning. They become active rather than passive learners.

This chapter described student-centered learning as it relates to assessment and discussed background information about negotiable contracting and student-generated rubrics. Several models of guiding students through the rubric-creating process were presented. Self-assessment and peer assessment were discussed, and guidelines for implementation were provided.

REFERENCES

Ainsworth, L., and Christinson, J. (1998). *Student-generated rubrics: An assessment model to help all students succeed.* Orangeburg, NY: Dale Seymour.

Anderson, R. S. (1998). Why talk about different ways to grade? The shift from traditional assessment to alternative assessment. In R. S. Anderson and B. W. Speck (Eds.), *Changing the way we grade student performances: Classroom assessment and the new paradigm* (pp. 5–16). San Francisco: Jossey-Bass.

Andrade, H. G. (1997). Understanding rubrics. *Educational Leadership,* 54(4), 44–48.

Harman, N. (2001). Student implementation of the rubric. In G. L. Taggart, S. J. Phifer, J. A. Nixon, and M. Wood (Eds.), *Rubrics: A handbook for construction and use* (pp. 37–44). Lanham, MD: Scarecrow Press.

Jensen. E. (2005). *Teaching with the brain in mind.* 2ed. Alexandria, VA: ASCD.

Lemov, D. (2010). *Teach like a champion.* San Francisco, CA: Jossey-Bass.

McCombs, B. L., and Whisler, J. S. (1997). *The learner-centered classroom and school: Strategies for increasing student motivation and achievement.* San Francisco, CA: Jossey-Bass.

Rhem, J. (1996). Urgings and cautions in student-centered teaching. *National Teaching and Learning Forum,* 5(4). Retrieved June 27, 2005 from www.ntlf.com/html/pi/9605/ article1.htm.

Rolheiser, C.and Ross, J. A.(n.d.). Student self-evaluation: What research says and what practice shows. Center for Development and Learning. Retrieved February 15, 2011 from www.cdl.org/resource-library/articles/self_eval.php.

Skillings, M. J., and Ferrell, R. (2000). Student-generated rubrics: Bringing students into the assessment process. *Reading Teacher,* 53(6), 452–55.

Stix, A. (1997, 2002). Creating rubrics through negotiable contracting. In C. Boston (Ed.), (2002). *Understanding scoring rubrics: A guide for teachers* (pp. 66–71). College Park, MD: ERIC Clearinghouse on Achievement and Evaluation.

Chapter 12

Using Rubrics in the Real World

An idealist is one who, on noticing that a rose smells better than a cabbage, concludes that it will also make a better soup.

—*H.L. Mencken*

There is a frequent debate among educators concerning theory versus practical application. Idealist educators, who are concerned with theories, often seem to avoid the real world dilemmas of the classroom in their advice to teachers. Teachers in the day-to-day classroom want practical strategies and situations that will make their lives easier while helping their students to learn. So it is in the world of scoring rubrics. Practitioners often challenge the idealists by asking how the scores on a rubric can be converted to report card grades.

Ideally, the transition from rubric to report card grading would be smooth and uneventful. However, grading traditions, as well as district or university policies, urge us to use alphabetic letters or percents as a means of reporting student achievement. These grading traditions are well established and are difficult to change.

For example, when total anecdotal report cards were implemented in grades K–3 of a local private school, parents were quick to complain. Their major concern was being able to present their children's report cards at a local fast-food restaurant to earn a cheeseburger if there was at least one *A* or *O* on the report card. Without the letter grade, how could they earn that burger? The problem was resolved by a quick call to the restaurant's manager, which enabled students to receive the free cheeseburger for good comments on the card.

Converting rubric scores to the real-world accountability of letter grades is not as difficult as one may believe. This chapter deals with the practicality of converting rubric scores to anecdotal comments, to letter grades, and to percentages for report cards. It illustrates how teachers are doing this and provides comments from veteran and novice rubric users. Issues of grading "effort" and zero scoring are addressed.

CONVERTING RUBRICS TO ANECDOTAL COMMENTS

If a school does not use letter grades—and perhaps even if it does—teachers probably spend a great deal of time writing anecdotal notes on report cards. One of the advantages of maintaining checklists, performance lists, and rubrics regularly is that teachers can develop a set of comments on which they can draw at report-card time. If these items are filed in student portfolios, they can become rich sources of information for teacher comments.

The narrative on report cards or letters to parents can be based on the rubric criteria by either repeating or summarizing the criteria. Comparing two or more scoring rubrics for the same child can demonstrate growth. Based on this evidence, the comments on the report card can be positive and encouraging by always emphasizing what the student *can* do.

For example, the writing checklist in chapter 2 would be a source of rich evidence for comments about a student's general writing ability as well as the areas of mechanics, conventions, and process. The measurement rubric in box 3.1 helps teachers to recall student development in specific skills, such as the ability to measure with non-standard items, to use a ruler correctly, to use correct measurement vocabulary, to complete activities at the math center, and to work independently.

The math rubric for primary grades in chapter 3 uses descriptors such as "completes task without assistance; uses verbal skills effectively; demonstrates flexibility in thinking; demonstrates understanding of concept." Even the homework rubrics as illustrated in boxes 4.2 and 5.2 provide a foundation for positive comments concerning organization and work habits to use on report cards or for parent conferences.

CONVERTING RUBRIC SCORES
TO REPORT CARD GRADES

Making the leap from the wording used in rubrics and checklists to anecdotal comments on the report card is relatively simple. More complicated is the leap from a rubric score to percentages or letter grades. Taking a 3, 2, or 1 and equating it with an *A, B, C, D,* or *F* can be challenging. However, educators are doing this more frequently with great success.

A listing of the procedures that educators have used to transfer rubric scores into reportable grades is shown in box 12.1. Details for each method are provided below the box.

Box 12.1 Eight Ways Rubrics Are Converted to Report Card Grades

- *Simple point conversion*—Use the basic 3-, 4- or 5-point rubric and convert those points to letter grades and record as such.
- *Range of points conversion*—Provide a range of *total* points and convert those ranges to letter grades or percentages.
- *Point averaging*—Average the levels of quality, either formally or informally.
- *Calculating percents*—Use the total sum of the possible *benchmark* points as the 100 percent.
- *Including point variations in the rubric*—Create rubrics with descriptors that assign various point amounts of each trait of the assignment. The total possible points are equal to the sum of the trait values.
- *Totaling the points*—Record the total number of possible points of each rubric assignment and the points earned by each student in the grading period and calculate the total percent.
- *Using technology*—Search for apps and websites that are available to do the math for you. Two examples can be found at www.roobrix.com and Android for Apps at http://androidforacademics.com/grade-rubric/
- *Redoing the report card*—Create a new report card format that is based on the standards and rubrics.

POINT CONVERSIONS

The most obvious conversion for some teachers is to take the basic four-point rubric (4, 3, 2, 1, 0) and convert those points to letter grades. Remembering that the three is the score that meets the standard for proficiency, teachers usually determine that a score of three would equal an *A*. A curriculum specialist relayed the belief that once teachers get over the shock that a score of one point can actually be satisfactory and passing, they become more comfortable in analyzing all work (Miller, n.d.).

However, for the practical teacher, using a five-point rubric where the five is beyond expectations and four is the benchmark, the 4.0 would be an *A*. This is the most simple.

Other teachers use a range of points earned on an analytic rubric to assign letter grades. This can be illustrated by the analytic rubric for a speech in box 2.7. This rubric actually provides a space for totals and teachers can inform students the range for grades. For example, a 15 or 16 point speech would be beyond expectations. A speech that earned 12 to 14 points would be a solid *A*, while other point ranges for letter grades would be based on the teacher's discretion and objectives.

A more precise mathematical way to calculate grades from an *analytic rubric* is to divide the total points earned by the number of categories in the analytic rubric (# of points earned ÷ # of categories) to yield a number between zero and four. Teachers can create their own range of numbers for letter grades. An example for a four-point rubric would be: A + = 4.0; A = 3.00 – 3.99; B = 2.25 – 2.90; C = 1.51 – 2.24; D = 0.81 – 1.50; and F = 0.0 – 0.80

For example, a 4-point analytic rubric with seven categories would have the total number of points earned divided by seven. A student who scores 22 points total would earn a 3.14 (22 ÷ 7) which would be an A. Someone who earned a total of 16 points would earn a 2.29 (16 ÷ 7) for a B.

A five-point analytic rubric categories would yield numbers between 5.0 and zero and may be graded as A + = 5.00; A = 4.00 – 4.90; B = 3.99 – 3.00; C = 2.99 – 2.00; D = 1.99 – 1.00; and below 1.00 would earn an F. Again, this is guided by teacher discretion.

POINT AVERAGING

Andrade (1997) reports that, "Because one piece of work rarely falls in only one level of quality, many teachers average out the levels of quality, either formally or informally" (p. 48).

An example of this type of levels-of-quality averaging would be using the points earned on the holistic rubric for a persuasive speech as illustrated in box 2.6. The three-point benchmark trait areas of volume, clarity, grammar and content are described, and the student who earns a three would be considered an *A* presentation; the score of four would earn an *A plus;* the two would be the *B*, while the one point could transfer as a *C* or *D* depending on the evaluator's conclusion.

Informal averaging is always reflected in a teacher's judgment. Teachers are quick to realize that students often meet criteria in two different levels. Continuing to use the holistic persuasive speech rubric as an example, a student may be loud enough for most to hear, articulate, and easy to understand (listed under three points), but have more than three grammatical errors (a two-point descriptor), and convince no one (a one-point descriptor).

An informal averaging of this work would yield a grade between a *B* and *C*. The teacher's decision of *B minus* or *C plus* might be based on the objective of the assignment. If the emphasis of the assignment was to persuade, then the lower score (*C plus)* would be appropriate, since the student obviously did not accomplish this. However, if the main objective was to improve public speaking skills, perhaps the higher score of a *B minus* would be awarded.

Using the averaging technique with an analytic rubric is less complicated than with the holistic rubric. The same persuasive speech assignment as evaluated in an analytic rubric will yield numerical scores in four areas: volume, clarity, grammar and content. Adding up the total points and dividing by 4 will yield a formal average between 4 and one. The zero would be for the student who did not participate.

CALCULATING PERCENTS

Teachers who are required to have percentage grades often use the total sum of the possible benchmark points as the 100 percent. In continuing the example of the persuasive speech, four benchmark categories are listed (volume, clarity, grammar, and content). Earning a three in each category will result in 12 points, which is the basis to use for calculating percentages. (Remember that the 3 points represents a solid understanding. Using the 16 as the basis will make for an unfair measure in calculating percents.)

Total points divided by 12 will yield the percentage. An example of the points and resulting percentages for this rubric are: an eleven-point presentation is a 92 percent (11 divided by 12), a ten is an 83 percent, nine points is 75 percent, and an eight will be a 67 percent. Anything over 12 will yield a percentage over 100.

As with any small number of points, percentage scoring tends to be severe. However, because of this limitation, teachers can be comfortable in being generous in the scoring. A *suggested* percentage range used successfully by one middle school teacher is:

86–100 = A
70–85 = B
45–69 = C
20–44 = D
0–19 = F

Teachers often reserve the right to adjust scores with plusses or minuses as they see fit.

POINT VARIATIONS INCLUDED IN THE RUBRIC

Teachers who prefer to use percentages as scores create their rubrics with descriptors that assign points to each trait of the assignment. The total possible points are equal to the sum of the trait values. An example of this scoring is shown in box 2.4, the science cell song performance list. In this rubric, the total value of the project is one hundred points and each component has a point value.

Because the teacher used 100 points as the total value, the student's total score is also equivalent to a percentage. However, even if the total were not 100, percentages could still be determined as with any point value assessment.

TOTALING THE POINTS

Another way of converting rubric scores into report card letter or percentage grades is by simply keeping track of the total number of points earned in the grading period and calculating the total percent. For some districts, the percentage grading scale is determined. Other teachers make their own decisions as to what percentages equal what letter grades. Some decide 90 to 100 percent is an *A*; 80 to 89 percent is a *B* and so on. Others are tougher with 93 or even 94 percent of total possible points earning the *A*.

Whatever percentages are used, teachers who use four-point or six-point rubrics are wise to remember to calculate total possible points *based on the benchmark* and not the exemplary or "beyond expectations" amount. In addition, teachers are urged to inform students and their parents of the assessment methods (Sadler, 2005).

REPORT CARDS USING RUBRICS

There is no single "best" way to manipulate rubric scores to become traditional *A* to *F* letter grades on report cards. However, school districts that have discovered the functionality and practicality of using scoring rubrics to assess standards-based education have worked diligently to create credible assessment reports for parents. The elementary report card created by a school district in New England can serve as a model for districts that are interested in constructing a similar assessment. Their experience resulted in the report card rubric illustrated in box 12.2.

Box 12.2 Sample Report Card Rubric

"Exceeds the standard" is not equal to a traditional "A." The mark "Exceeds the Standard" will be very rare and should be reserved for exceptional and consistent *attainment of standards. The expectation is that most students will end the year with a grade of "Meets the Standard."*

E Exceeds the standard

The student demonstrates thorough, in-depth understanding of basic and extended concepts and skills. Performance is characterized by self-motivation and the ability to apply the skills with consistent accuracy, independence, and a high level of quality.

M Meets the standard

The student demonstrates thorough understanding of basic concepts and skills. Performance is characterized by the ability to apply the skills with accuracy, quality, and independence.

P Progressing toward the standard

The student demonstrates understanding of basic concepts and skills. Performance is characterized by the ability to apply skills with increasing success. Performance varies in consistency with regard to accuracy and quality. Support and guidance often needed for clarification and to sustain involvement.

B Beginning to develop the standard

The student demonstrates minimal understanding of basic concepts and skills. Performance is inconsistent even with support and guidance.

———— Standard not addressed this term

Reprinted with permission: Franklin Public Schools, Franklin, MA, 2005, 2011.

The report card actually has a list of the required standards and teachers assess each student's ability to meet the standard with the following criteria:

> *E* for exceeds the standard
> *M* for meeting the standard
> *P* for progressing toward the standard
> *B* for beginning to develop

The dash indicates that the standard is not being assessed at the time of reporting (Franklin Public Schools, 2005, 2011).

The detailed criteria paragraphs that describe each score in detail are clear and precise and are included on each report card. The disclaimer used is an excellent explanation that the highest grade of *E* is not comparable to the traditional *A* and states the expectation that most students will meet the standard (*M*) with independence by the end of the school year.

Creating this tool took time, dedication, and cooperation. The administrators, teachers, and parents worked together through focus groups for about two years to determine the terminology and format that would be clear, concise, and accurate. Their success is evident. Not only is the report card rubric a tool of information for parents, it also helps teachers to focus on appropriate skills and objectives to meet the required standards. When reflecting on the former *A, B, C, D, F* report card, the stakeholders of this district agreed that they would "never want to go back."

ZEROS AND RUBRICS

Teachers frequently disagree on the awarding of zeros. The dispute regularly centers on the inability of students to raise their scores out of the hole that a zero creates. This is obviously true on an assignment of 50 to 100 points. Teachers who use traditional rubrics of three or four points usually have no difficulty with this problem. Because the score of zero has been described and is reserved for the empty page, students who are aware of this usually manage to submit something. It is also much easier for a student to recover from a zero in an assignment that is worth three or nine points than the 100- or 50-point deficit.

GRADING EFFORT

Another area open for debate is the inclusion of "effort" in evaluating students. Educators differ on the importance that effort plays in assessing student work. The difference of opinion is based on the grading of pure academics versus including points for student's diligent hard work, which includes effort and improvement.

Again, teachers who use scoring rubrics can comfortably include an area of effort into their rubrics. This can be a separate rubric or one component of an analytic rubric. School districts often create a section of their report cards to address effort and improvement, which requires documentation.

A suggested description of a rubric to assess effort might be:

- Consistently (90–100% of the time) demonstrates effort in work
- Usually (70–89% of the time) demonstrates effort in work
- Sometimes (50–69% of the time) demonstrates effort in work
- Seldom (less than half the time) demonstrates effort in work.

WHAT TEACHERS AND STUDENTS ARE SAYING

Those who use rubrics in education are quite vocal about implementing rubrics in the classroom. Their comments are self explanatory:

"I started using rubrics about 12–13 years ago when I was teaching language arts to eighth graders. I enjoyed doing projects with novels, but hated grading a typical book report because it just seemed so subjective. I started looking into various forms of assessment and how to grade projects.

"At that time, rubrics were not a 'hot topic.' I made my own for the various projects and simply used them for my benefit. As that year progressed, I started having the children help to design the rubric prior to the project being assigned and allowing them to have the rubric upfront. Wow! What a difference this made in the end results. When I talked to the classes and asked what made them improve, most said, well, they knew what was expected. That year was a very powerful experience for me as a teacher" (Elementary administrator).

"What came next was quite a surprise to me. The students [fourth grade] were discussing rubrics. I never knew what a rubric was when I was in elementary school. In fact, I only recently learned what it was!" (Graduate student's observation of fourth grade)

"She [the classroom teacher] helped me so much making a rubric for my lesson. She believes that in order to have a great lesson, you have to know how you are going to evaluate your students and knowing that helps you write your lesson and objectives" (Student teacher in grade three).

"I never assign a project without handing out the rubric right along with it. It makes my life so much simpler" (Middle school teacher).

"When Mrs. Smith gives me the rubric, it makes me feel like I can do the work" (Special education student with identified learning disability).

"It [the rubric] makes it easy to know what I have to do for an *A* "(Gifted student in fifth grade).

"When the rubric is specific, it clarifies the expectations for my child" (Parent of an eighth-grader).

"I have now developed a form which enables me to systematically evaluate each facet of the assignment. I have found that doing this helps me to answer many questions students have about why received a certain grade. Also, when I show students the form that will be used to evaluate their work ahead of time, I find that the quality of their assignments improves" (High school teacher).

"It is amazing that after 20 years we can still continue learning how to be more effective in our teaching! . . . When, in a given semester, a number of students fail to meet one of my criteria for an assignment, I try to find ways to state my expectations more clearly the next time around" (College professor).

From a non-teacher, "By the way, I've incorporated customer service rubrics for my staff (I supervisor over 30 people) and although there was some initial resistance, it's actually helped to increase performance evaluation scores because they know what's expected and graded. So, plus one to rubrics in the 'real world,' too!"

And for those of you who are feeling guilty about *not* using a rubric: "My students prefer the preciseness and fairness of grading with a rubric; however, sometimes not using a rubric and just 'grading with my gut' can be so liberating" (College professor).

SUMMARY

Teachers generally recognize the value of using rubrics to assess student work and as a basis for anecdotal comments to parents. However, many are concerned about how they can manage the transformation of rubric scores into reportable grades. Since there is no single best method for converting rubric scores into report card grades, educators are encouraged to choose from a variety of techniques that practicing teachers have used successfully to translate rubric scores into anecdotal comments, letter grades, or percentages.

This chapter has dealt with the practicality of converting rubric scores to anecdotal comments and to grades and percentages for report cards. It illustrated seven methods that educators use to convert rubrics to report card scores or grade sheets. Issues of grading effort and awarding zeroes were addressed. Comments from veteran and novice rubric users were provided.

REFERENCES

Andrade, H. G. (1997). Understanding rubrics. *Educational Leadership*, 54(4), 44–48.
Clauson, D. J. (1998). How rubrics become grades. *Mathematics Teaching in the Middle School*, 4(2), 118–19.

Franklin Public Schools (2005, 2011). Elementary report card marking descriptors. Retrieved: May 19, 2011: franklin.ma.us/auto/schools/oak/classrooms/buchheister/rubrics/guidelines.htm.

Mathews, J. (June 14, 2005). Where some give credit, others say it's not due. *Washington Post,* A-10.

Miller, C. (n.d.). *How to turn rubric scores into grades.* Retrieved May 15, 2011: www.intercom.net/local/school/sdms/mspap/grading.html.

Sadler, D. R. (2005). Interpretation of criteria-based assessment and grading in higher education. *Assessment & Evaluation in Higher Education,* 30(2), 175–94.

Appendix

RUBRIC WEBSITES

This is a listing of websites devoted to scoring rubrics and rubric related activities. They have been categorized by use. Sites that required fees to subscribe were excluded.

At the time of publication, all of the website addresses (URLs) were checked for availability and accuracy.

However, some sites on the web have a short shelf life and disappear without warning. Lost sites often can be relocated by typing in the name of the site into a search engine such as Google or Yahoo.

Another resource for lost sites is to use the "Way Back Machine" website at www.archive.org/index.php to locate the change of address locations. At this site, you simply type in the old URL and it takes you to the new address if available.

Banks of Rubrics with Multiple Subject Areas

- Variety of rubrics in all subjects are available from the Alaska Department of Education: www.eed.state.ak.us/tls/frameworks/arts/6assess3 .htm#samplerubric
- The Rubric Bank of Chicago Public schools contains rubrics for reading, math, science, social studies, fine arts, speaking, and writing for all grade levels: www.cps.edu/Results.aspx?k=rubrics

- Kathy Schrock's Guide for Rubrics site includes graphic organizers and report cards along with rubrics: school.discovery.com/schrockguide/assess.html
- Rubrics 4 Teachers includes a wide variety of current and archived rubrics: www.rubrics4teachers.com/
- Special education rubrics from Bethlehem Central School District, NY: bcsd.k12.ny.us/specialeducation/rubrics.html

Specific Subject Area Rubrics

- Comparison rubric to assess students' ability to compare and contrast can be found: www.psych.westminster.edu/inquiry1g/comparison_rubric.html
- Critical thinking rubrics appropriate for gifted education Hawaii Public Schools: doe.k12.hi.us/curriculum/GLO_rubric_grade1–6.htm
- Family and consumer sciences and fine arts, including dance: www.uen.org/Rubric/browse.cgi
- Inference rubric for middle school: www.middleweb.com/ReadWrkshp/RWdownld/InferRubric2.pdf
- Kindergarten language arts checklist: www.geocities.com/Athens/Oracle/8314/grkinla.htm
- Project Based Learning provides checklists on writing, oral presentations, science, and multimedia in both English and Spanish: pblchecklist.4teachers.org/checklist.shtml
- SAT Scoring Guide SAT Scoring Guide: www.collegeboard.com/student/testing/sat/about/sat/essay_scoring.html
- Technology evaluation of websites with multiple links www.siec.k12.in.us/~west/online/eval.htm

Behavior/Homework Rubrics

- Rubric links are provided including one to generate a behavior modification rubric: www.lessonplansearch.com/Rubrics/

Rubric Building Sites

- Rubistar is a free tool to help teachers develop quality rubrics: rubistar.4teachers.org/index.php
- Teacher-created rubrics-maker with a range of subjects including art and music: teach-nology.com/web_tools/rubrics/
- Utah Education Network includes family and consumer sciences, fine arts, etc.

Can use "as is" or customize for specific needs: www.uen.org/Rubric/browse.cgi

Miscellaneous:

- Multiple links to a variety of Internet projects for all grade levels with and without rubrics: www.internetschoolhouse.com/
- This site has teacher comments on rubrics, lets you read what other teachers are saying, and invites teachers to join the discussion: www.middleweb.com/MWLISTCONT/MSLrubrics.html
- An automatic calculator for converting rubrics to percentages or letter grades. roobrix.com/

Index

About the Author

Audrey M. Quinlan is currently the chair of the Division of Education and director of the master's program in elementary education at Seton Hill University in Greensburg, Pennsylvania. Dr. Quinlan has taught grades K–12 in both public and parochial schools, has also served as an elementary and middle school principal, and has conducted workshops on creating scoring rubrics, storytelling, conflict resolution, and brain-based teaching and learning. She currently teaches undergraduate and graduate methods courses in elementary math, as well as online courses on brain-based teaching at Seton Hill University. She and her husband have two children and three grandsons.